OUR TABLE OF MEMORIES

OUR TABLE OF MEMORIES:

Food and Poetry of Spirit, Homeland and Tradition

A collaborative project with the STORIES OF ARRIVAL:
REFUGEE & IMMIGRANT YOUTH VOICES POETRY PROJECT
and PROJECT FEAST

EDITED BY MERNA ANN HECHT

PUBLISHED BY CHATWIN BOOKS FOR THE STORIES OF ARRIVAL PROJECT

Stories of Arrival: Youth Voices Poetry Project
Merna Ann Hecht, founder, editor
mernaanna@yahoo.com

4
CULTURE

ISBN: 978-1-63398-033-4
Corrected printing, 2016

Published by Chatwin Books for the Stories of Arrival project.

For orders and inquiries:

Chatwin Books
Seattle, Washington
www.chatwinbooks.com

Dedication

To the spirited words of our poets.

To bringing poetry forth from all young people
where the silence remains too loud.

And to the possibility of a world where no child is hungry.

Contents

Project Partners

Our poetry project is a partnership project between Seattle's Jack Straw Cultural Center, The Institute for Poetic Medicine in Palo Alto, CA, the Tukwila School District, Foster High School, and KBCS 91.3 FM Radio. The Stories of Arrival: Youth Voices Poetry Project has been a 501 c-3 Shunpike-affiliated project since November, 2013.

Introduction

The Stories of Arrival: Refugee & Immigrant Youth Voices Poetry Project and Project Feast—a New Collaboration

Our Table of Memories: Food and Poetry of Spirit, Homeland and Tradition reflects our camaraderie with Project Feast in celebrating our shared values as to what sustains and nourishes us. We invite you to consider the delicious connections between food, poetry and stories within this book. Among our greatest hopes for the book is that it will foster broader understandings of and deep respect for King County's diverse refugee and immigrant communities who have made this area their home.

We believe that our community is made stronger when the voices of those who are not often heard are more widely celebrated. We join with Project Feast in their wish to "prove that the very difficult circumstances that result from forced migration and immigration are not insurmountable." In each of our programs one of our goals is to expand the presence of our participants into the community— and thus this first-time collaboration and the excitement of our newly released book!

The Stories of Arrival Poetry Project takes place at Foster High School, one of the most language diverse high schools in the country. Many of the participants were forced out of their countries and lived in refugee camps before arriving in the U.S. They all hope to pursue a high quality education that will allow them to reach their dreams and goals for a better life. Our students are English Language Learners; most have never written poetry before this project. Their outpourings of deeply emotional and image-rich poetry are a testament to both the power of poetic expression and to the indelible imprint of memories from their homelands.

Project Feast, located in the Tukwila Community Center, a short distance from Foster High School, serves refugee and immigrant women. Their mission is to "transform the lives of refugees and immigrants by providing pathways to sustainable employment in the local food industry and to enrich communities through exploring ethnic culture and cuisine." Our collaboration has allowed us to create intergenerational connections between our students and Project Feast participants all for the good purpose of demonstrating the remarkable power of food and of poetry to bring people to the table to foster mutual understandings across cultures.

I believe the world is beautiful
And that poetry, like bread, is for everyone.

—Roque Dalton, El Salvadoran poet

I have learned that every culture has
their own food and their own story to tell.

—Project Poet, from Somalia

A Note from Merna Ann Hecht

Project Founder, Co-director, Teaching Artist, and Book Editor

For the past six years it has been an honor for me to work with young refugees and immigrants from many different parts of the world. Their stories, many of which involve harrowing struggles, are also important stories of hope. The privilege of observing the vision and creativity of these young people and understanding first-hand how much they have to contribute to all of our lives has been a source of inspiration to me. Poets and peace-makers, they have learned how poetry transcends the daunting task of expressing oneself in a new language. They have taken up pens and pencils, spoken with honesty and vulnerability, and discovered their own pathways for bringing the language of their hearts to the page.

This year, in collaboration with Project Feast, our students have crafted poems drawing from memories of food in their homelands. For all of us it has been a fascinating culinary journey. As I poured through the students' recipes, I was struck by how each family seems to have its own way of preparing a dish common to its region. Such particularity serves to remind us there can be no single lens for understanding the often minute details of difference within families and cultural traditions. Food is sustenance, but it is also a transport back to homelands, grandparents, childhood and important rituals that define and express who we are.

Recently, one of the students in our poetry project said, "When we began the project, we were students, but now we are poets." And it is true. Poem after poem evokes memories of place and all that flourishes there— gardens, family and community bonds, cultural traditions and sacred festivals. These poems abound with bright flavors, but they are not without the bitter tastes of hunger and warfare. A pomegranate becomes a symbol for the taste of war with the line, *the red of the blood, like the color of a pomegranate*. A poem about a cucumber in the poet's homeland ends with deep emotion, *Goodbye to you, cucumber of my country / I will remember that sunset over you, / like two halves of a once whole heart*. From writing about the taste of a lemon in a home country comes the lines, *When I eat lemons, my soul gets rest / and it brings me power over myself*. And the last stanza in a poem in praise of rice bestows the rice with a persona, *I want to walk into your fields / I want to stand there with you far from the white tablecloth / I want to fill my hands with the mud of your fields / like a blessing*.

Our young poets have used words to stir up images and memories much like nourishing food comes to us fresh from a garden, prepared with love and spiced with surprises. A sense of communal belonging and an understanding that we must tend to the earth, its creatures and each other, are present in many of the poems. And still these poems speak to sorrow and loss. They speak of how violence, scarcity and hunger tear families apart, threaten survival and silence our songs of praise. Praise for our sustenance is one of the most ancient forms of poetry and has long been part of the human story. But, as these young poets in their remarkable wisdom already know, we are living in an extraordinary time. A time when farmers' fields and gardens are under threat; when food is inundated with chemicals, over-processed and corporatized; and when language is used and abused, to marginalize, to justify closing borders and to dehumanize those who struggle to survive.

Every young person in this project and each woman we have met through Project Feast is an ambassador for teaching us about the courage required to endure the ache of leaving a homeland. They inspire us as they find their way, using a new language and adjusting to this vastly different country. Even so, the Project Feast cooks and our young poets tell us they will always miss the taste of home.

The guiding vision of a table where we can break bread together with a spirit of gratitude has prompted us to create this book so that Project Feast cooks and our poets can bring you the many cultural traditions that continue to enrich our own country. Our students have been passionate in their poetry, reflecting back to us that poems can reach places within us that seem unsayable about who we are, about what and whom we have lost, and about what we hope for. Poetry can nourish us like the food that sustains us and connects us to others in profoundly intimate ways—the very foundation on which Project Feast is built and the bedrock of our possibilities for peace and for caretaking the earth and each other.

—Merna Ann Hecht
Project Founder, Co-director,
Teaching Artist, and Book Editor

A Note from Carrie Stradley

FOSTER HIGH SCHOOL ELL TEACHER, PROJECT CO-DIRECTOR

What has brought you, the reader here to share in the experiences of immigrant and refugee youth today is undoubtedly a deep desire to understand others who are frequently misrepresented or misunderstood. It is with this same intention that we conceived this Project. Thank you for supporting the students of the Stories of Arrival Poetry Project and the participants of Project Feast by thoughtfully considering their poems and recipes.

Inside this anthology is not merely a unit of poetry carved out of a school year, but the opportunity to bear witness and honor the lives of these incredible youth. Throughout the project I have witnessed my students grow in their willingness to share of themselves, in their command of the English language, and in their ever-evolving identities of themselves in the landscape of a new country. Not only did they develop the fine art of crafting poetry by deliberating over word choice, but also they have experienced a new way to use their voices with expression rather than the utilitarian English they use to navigate high school.

A single test can never show the impact this work has had on them, and its positive effects will last much longer. I'm honored and humbled to work with these remarkable youth, who have shared with us so generously excerpts of their own lives so that we might be reminded how poetry transports culture and serves to record the humanity in history.

Carrie Stradley, NBCT
ELL Teacher and Co-director

Our Immense Appreciation to These Generous Individuals:

Karen and Philip Cushman
Linda Flinn
Cal Kinnear
Katy Jo Steward
M. Vandenberg
Sam and Lisa Verhovek
Edward "Skip" Walter

Wendell Tangborn & Andrea Lewis
Rob Crawford
James Dubinsky
Laura Gamache
Sarah Robinson Greenthal
Elizabeth Norville
Stephen Silha
Sarah Stuart

Judit Arnold, MD
Marta E. Bull
Sitka Gatto
Wendy Lustbader & Barry Grosskopf
Jan Rosenberg
Jeanne Rosenberg
Rolf Gruen
Joan Hanna
Janie & Kirk Starr
Kristin Tregillus
Christine Zimmer

Terry Blackhawk

Jeri Jo Carstairs
Jane Dunbar
Gerri Haynes
Debbie Hecht Reier
Deborah Hyman
Christine Smith
Amy Watkins & Christopher Szala
Kimberly Whitson
Anne Mulherkar, Young Writers Workshop
Paul Zimmerman

Debbie McVay Aldous
Diane Banner
Valerie Bowman
Kaori Brand
Sally Fox
Erica Rose Englund
David Hassler
Fong Hoonan
Jeri Kuoppamaki
Terry Lawhead
Stacy LeMelle
Judy Michaels
Rachel Payne
Emily Safer
Ginger Shephard
Celia Fulton Walden
Joanna Wright

We are grateful for the generosity of these individual donors. Our apologies to any donors who are not listed here because their donations were received after we went to press.

The Food of My Country: Memories & Traditions

Corn Soup

JAMES MUNG

In our family tradition
corn soup is *value*.
One evening
in our Tukwila home,
I saw corn soup
at my mom's kitchen table,

Like missing my country,
the corn soup tastes
like memories of my grandparents
in their village, in Burma,
the corn soup symbolizes living
together, each one of us in peace.

When I close my eyes
I smell the sweetness of my mom
cooking her corn soup,
it is like seeing my goal
before I achieve it.

Sel Roti*

SAGAR RAI

Devouring ten Sel Roti outside my house in Nepal
sitting next to the mango trees,
their dark green leaves shading me,
seeing my friends pretending to gamble like elders with rupees,
dogs trying to find another meal,
a new mom holding her baby,
hearing a father yell at his son
telling him to stop smoking,

If I could go back in time
I would tell myself
to live as long as you can
to keep a smile on your face
to always love everyone
to laugh for a reason,
to show who you are
to do something your heart tells you
to show people that you can always be respectful
to make your family and your people proud of you
to remember the world is made of love
to be trusting, to help all people
even your enemies.

If I could go back in time
I would tell myself all of these things,
and I would tell myself
to share ten Sel roti with my friends.

Sel roti (Nepali: सेल रोटी) is a Nepali traditional home-made, sweet, ring-shaped rice bread/doughnut. It is mostly prepared during Tihar, a widely celebrated Hindu festival in Nepal. It is made of rice flour with added customized flavors. (Wikipedia).

How Is It Possible?

MALAAK ABDALLAH

I don't know
how it is possible
that we have one universe,
7 oceans, and 195 countries,
but food tastes different
from land to land
fruit and vegetables
have an after taste
that is otherworldly, different.

In Ethiopia, the potatoes seem
dry, brown and lifeless
they taste stale,
like the iron pills I took
for anemia,
not like the fresh Somali potatoes
from my grandmother's farm.

And the Ethiopian enjera with the sauce
like a volcano, so spicy
that hot tears stream down your cheeks
and the meat that tastes to me
of a cotton ball dipped in water,
but, for me, my Somali enjera is bright,
with lamb liver, with onions,
garlic, spices and fresh herbs.

In Kenya, the mashed semolina is hard as a rock,
not like the Somali semolina,
soft like mashed potatoes,
or as soft as *shash** made for the first day
of a girl's wedding.

In America, the pumpkin cake
should not be covered in so much saccharine,
it is not like the spongy vanilla cake
that my mother made with love.

I have learned that every culture
has their own food
and their own story to tell.

**Married women in Somalia tend to sport head-scarves
referred to as* shash. *Unmarried or young women, how-
ever, do not always cover their heads.*

For Malaak's Somali Tea recipe, see page 143.

Las manos de mi padre

NATHALY ROSAS

Recuerdo las manos de mi padre
Poniendo una manzana roja cada mañana
En mis manos
Deseándome un buen dia en la escuela
Delicadamente limpiaba la manzana para mi

A veces pensaba que sus manos tenían la esencia
De el perfume de mi madre
Ella me abrazaba cada vez
Que se iba a trabajar
A veces las manos de mi padre se sentían como las suaves manos
De mi pequeño hermano tomando mi mano
De camino a nuestro hogar después de escuela

Cuantas memorias puede guardar una simple manzana
A veces el mundo revuela
Alrededor de esta pequeña manzana
Y no lo sabemos

Esta manzana a veces llora conmigo
Cuando recuerdo todas las cosas
Que me hacen sonreir
Los brazos chiquitos de mi hermano
Recordando las personas en mi vida
Mi padre, mis amigos, mi familia
Y estoy esperando a estar viva otra vez

My Father's Hands

NATHALY ROSAS

I remember my father's hands
Putting a red apple every morning
In my hands,
Wishing me a good day at school
Gently wiping the apple for me,

Sometimes I thought his hands had the scent
Of the perfume of my mother
She hugged me every time
Before going to work,
Sometimes my father's hands felt like the soft hands
Of my brother holding my hand
On my way home from school.

How many memories can save a simple apple?
Sometimes the world revolves
Around this small apple
And we don't know it.
This apple sometimes cries with me
When I remember all the things
That make me smile
Like the tiny arms of my brother.

Remembering the people in my life
My father, my friends, my family
They are waiting to be alive again.

For Nathaly's recipe for Mexican Quesadillas, see page 132.

Golden Days

AVNOOR BRAR

Memories of my country fill my heart,
Memories that we can no longer find,
Golden days of childhood.
Memories of my grandparents in India,
In the village Sri Gangaunagar 36F,
When my grandmother made me her different dishes—
Gulgule, Mall Purhe and *Saag,*
And my grandfather took me to the fields,
But those days will not come again in my life.

Still I picture in my mind
When I went to my grandparents' village
The sweet dishes my grandmother made,
My friend, Harjot who I played with, how we helped each other,

We have these memories that come again and again
But that time of childhood does not return,
The large, empty fields, the rainy days,
The golden days that will not return ever in our lives.

I Remember

RODAS NEGUSSIE

I remember the taste of injera in Ethiopia
soft, hot and delicious,
when I see injera it consumes my mind.
"Gursha" is how we feed each other in my country
we offer food two times,
one bite for respect,
and another bite for love.

I remember the taste of my grandmother's chicken stew,
simmering, with red *berbere* and yellow turmeric,
these foods take me back
to the highlands of Ethiopia
to the beauty of the green mountains,
white rivers and rich valleys.

I remember the sound of students singing
the national anthem, proud and fortunate
in my school in Ethiopia,
and I remember the smell of the roasted earthy
and rich birthplace of coffee.

I remember the sound of my mom's voice,
when she advised me to slow down in the garden
as I was running, because I was running too fast.
I remember all of this and feel safe,
and with these memories, my childhood quickly returns
to injera and coffee.

*For Rodas' recipe for Doro wet (chicken stew), with berbere spice, see page 120.

Limes with Friends

CECILIA DAWT IANG

It looks like sunshine,
smells like the jungle,
in Hakha Chin we cut it in pieces
seasoned with salt, *ngapi* and chili pepper,
it reminds me of my friends
Sui Hei, Melody, Esther
Sung Kalay, and Aung Aung,
when we built a small house in the jungle tree,
when we played hide and seek, and tag
running, jumping, joking and laughing.

When we were tired and took a rest
we sat in our small jungle tree house
hearing the sounds of birds
while eating the fresh limes.

For Cecilia's recipe for An ttam thor (Burmese Mustard Greens with Rice), see page 142.

Asian Pear

Susma Rai

Saturday afternoon
My friend and me
Heading to the bazar
To buy pears
To take them home and share
With Lalima and Rena.

The Asian Pear smells fresh and crisp,
Is it smooth like the calm lake in Pathri,
It tastes like a spring morning,
It is as crisp as an old dried mango leaf,
It is soft yellow
And reminds me of Nepal
When I was ten years old
When I went out at night
And stared out at the moon
And saw crisp star light
And felt I could do anything
At that time,
When my life was new.

Spicy Mango

THAN WIN

My father was born in Burma
my father moved to Thailand
so he could meet my mother,
my mother lived in Thailand
where I was born
my dad always had mangoes with him
it was like the mango was stuck to him.

After the war in Thailand, I lived in a refugee camp,
we always had the same after school snack,
my mother would make this every day
chili spice, with mango,
mango trees were waiting for me in the road
near my school and my house,
dark green leaves ,
light green, soft sticky fruit
on the tops of mango branches
looking just like the way they taste.
Mangoes can be eaten alone
or they can be for a party,
they can solve your problems,
make you shine like a diamond,
the taste makes you remember your love,
the spice is so hot
it makes your cheeks red, blushing.

For Than's recipe for Thai Fish Chowder, see page 126.

Leaving Kurdistan, Iraq

Madyan Bakr

We left Kurdistan, Iraq because of the war
it felt heartbreaking to leave,
we now live in Tukwila,
but Iraq, Kurdistan
I hold your food,
my culture's food
in my mind and heart,
like a child holding his mother's hands
crossing a busy street.

I grew up on this food,
when my mom makes
Tabsi for us
she folds in the meat,
chicken and tomatoes,
white onion and potatoes,
sometimes oil and eggplants
swimming in salt,
it reminds me of the old days
in my village, Shingal
solving my family's problems
over fresh *Tabsi*,
I love it,
almost more than anyone
in my family.

For Madyan's recipe for Doulmh (Iraqi Stuffed Grape Leaves), see page 117.

I Miss

SAMA JABBARIMEHMANI

I miss listening to the sound of my grandmother
excitedly telling stories of her childhood in old Iran
playing with her little sister in a flower garden in Tehran,
I miss helping my mom cook *Tahchin*
mixing the rice with saffron,
I miss smelling saffron
like fresh morning air
mixing with the yellow rising sun,
I miss listening to my uncle's jokes,
I miss watching comedy movies
with my cousin
laughing with my family
and eating popcorn.
Sometimes I just miss
my close friends
and traveling to the forest
and to the Caspian sea
where the sea is both shadow and sky.

For Sama's recipe for Sholeh Zard (Iranian Saffron Rice Pudding), see page 118.

Memories in a Lemon

Mahendra Biswa

In Nepal there was a refugee camp
called Khudunabari with beautiful
refugee people,

I remember me and my friends went
to a village to bring a treat of lentils
to the village people
so that they would give us more lemons.

When I eat lemons my soul gets rest
and it brings me power over myself,
but to find the lentils and trade them for lemons
we usually had to steal the lentils from our home
and in the night time our parents were angry enough
to beat us, but I still wanted the lentils to trade
because lemons are my life and my soul.

To me, lemons look like beautiful sunshine
in a blue sky,
to me, lemons feel like jack fruit
growing near the sea.

For Mahendra's recipe for Paleu (Nepalese Rice Pudding), see page 146.

Bamboo House

HELEN BOIH

I remember the Christmas songs
And holding the stick of corn with bamboo,
I remember preparing the corn,
First my mother would build up the fire
In the stove, then she put the corn on the grill
And moved it around slowly,
She turned the corn until it was done,
It smelled like warm morning air,
When I ate the corn, my mother told me,
You should learn how to cook, it will taste better
When you grow up.

When I was seven years old in Burma
My mother taught me how to cook,
First with rice water
Then I put it on the fire
And moved it around until the rice was done,
Then I learned to make vegetables,
Pumpkin leaf, potato leaf.

I miss my country, the land full
Of diverse and innocent people,
The smile on the children's faces,
The beautiful birds singing in the mornings,
And my beautiful bamboo house,
The color of the deep sunset,
The bamboo house of my heart.
I remember my bamboo house day by day
Like I would remember a beautiful flower,
Both of them have faded
And fallen away.

My bamboo house, I remember you
In the middle of the night when I woke up
And stood outside with the stars,
I would look up at the colorful sky
And I would see the stars,
And you were there.

Heaven Is a Pupusa

WILBERT ALEXANDER ANAYA MURCIA

My parents were born in El Salvador
my mom learned to make pupusas
a traditional food of El Salvador, pupusas
are made with corn flour, cheese and refried beans.

We often ate pupusas at the dinner table
with our family members
around the light brown table,
playing card games and laughing
like crazy, sharing stories and eating pupusas.

Pupusas were our weekend food
they have a deep flavor
like my parents expected of me.

Pupusas are easy to make
you can eat them every day
like my parents let me go out
every day to visit friends.

Pupusas have a strong smell
of melting cheese, fragrant and rich,
with a strong taste
like you're touching heaven.

Pupusas are not always a side dish,
but they are strong enough
to be eaten alone,
they can be independent
like me.

For Wilbert's recipe for Pupusas, see page 134.

My Village Food

NINI KHAING

Memories of my hometown near the beach,
and memories of eating *Kanom jeen*
fill my soul,
every Sunday the scent floated through my window
the days were full of butterflies
flying over the flowers
floating rocks over the ocean
clear road,
leaves were shining like night stars,
fruit was falling like golden flowers.

Kanom jeen has white skinny pasta
like a woman wearing a wedding gown,
it has small, bright green chilies
like plants that people cut down in the forest,
it has tiny round garlic, like cream that we put in tea.
We took fresh water,
like rain water streaming on the glass window,
we took that water from the nearby beach,
fresh clean water.

In Thailand, in everyday life we usually ate
rice, meat, fish, vegetables, and soup
and each day we added one dish called
Kanom jeen.

In each meal I remember, I can hear
my family laughing, talking,
giggling, and sharing,
not only did the people make our village warm,
but our food always made our village
near the beach more delightful.

*For Nini's recipe for Thai Shrimp Fried Rice,
see page 124.*

How is it Possible?

JEEWAN POUDEL

I remember when I was back in my country, Nepal,
when I was only three years old
when I planted a mango seed in my backyard,
but I did not take care of the tree
unit I was eight years old.

My family told me,
you forgot about that mango tree,
I didn't even remember planting it,
I planted only one seed, but two trees grew.

People used to come ask me
can I get a mango
म साधारण प्राप्त गर्न सक्छन्
I replied,
no you can't, this is my own mango tree,
कुनै तपाईं यो मेरो आफ्नै साधारण रूख छ सक्दैन
and when people came to buy them,
I still said no.

And when I left the mango tree
I was eleven years old,
and that tree was like my family.

If my mango tree is still alive in Nepal
I think it would look like a haunted tree,
a tree without its leaves, with only branches,
no mangoes, they would be on the ground
bruised and brown from falling,
rotting on the earth.

For Jeewan's recipe for Nepalese Kheer
(Rice Pudding), see page 144.

My Memories

Hy Cao

Memories of my best friend fill my mind,
Memories of Nhat,
I ate breakfast with him every day,
I went to school with him every day,
Every day we helped each other,
Sometimes he took care of me when I got sick.
Memories of a food that helped me live every day
That is rice, just rice
And there was also soup
That helped me live every day,
Soup with meat, vegetables, ginger and peanuts.
When I think of Ho Chi Minh City
I miss noodle soup and pho,
And I miss my red bicycle.

A Bowl of Steaming Pho

Vu Nguyen

A big bowl of pho
steam and heat coming to my face
hot, on a cold raining day.

Bones soaked for hours and hours,
make the soup sweeter
it brings out their marrow
to give us more energy,
the smell of star anise, cool.

Add some bean sprouts
Sriracha, hoisin sauce,
squeeze a piece of lemon
finally egg! um um,
this all makes the bowl more appealing,
"come here darling,"
I can hear myself in my head,
I can't wait any longer.

Take the spoon,
pick up the egg
carefully, carefully
scared the yolk will break,
take it to my mouth
then the yolk breaks,
flows into my mouth
I taste it, still so sweet,
smells good, doesn't it?!

Noodles are beautiful,
white, long and soft,
I pick up my chopsticks
blow and blow
slowly begin to eat
my hot bowl of pho
"that tuyet voi lam sao."

Our Lime

Julianna Moe

"Lime,"
just hearing the word
brings back a thousand
pieces of memories
of you, best friend of mine.

The smell of lime
is like fresh air after rain,
it feels like your soft hands,
like your smooth long hair
that waves through thin air.

It can remind me of your soft heart
that beats like a drum.
Best friend of mine, your warmth can heal
a thousand people from sickness.

Remember,
we used to cut out the lime,
put it inside the bowl with salt,
hot pepper, *ajinomoto* and *ngapi*.
You used to complain that
putting *ngapi* made its smell bad.

That spicy, hot lime made our tears
fall down over our faces,
we were bursting out laughing,
but we still ate all that hot lime.

Our precious memories
my memories being with you,
can't be forgotten,
can't be broken.
Our friendship is like a tattoo
that can't be erased.

That moment, I want to go back to,
but it's only a memory,
I can't go back to that time anymore,
it is long gone,
I miss you.
It's hard to describe how much,
I hope we will see
each other again.

For Julianna's recipe for Mohinga (Burmese Fish Noodle Soup), see page 140.

Cucumbers

Naina Rai

Cucumbers cut into slices
covered in chili and salt
in Nepal, in the refugee camp
my friends Sangeeta, Deepa, Hasu
and I loved to eat cucumbers
in the hot afternoons,
we sat on a bench
talking about movies and dreams,
the cucumbers tasted
like sweet water
unless we ate them with chili and salt.
When I think of my friends
I miss my country, Nepal.

When I think of Nepal,
I dream of returning
to visit my friends and family,
I would like to eat Nepali food
made by the hands of my auntie
who took care of me like a mother.

Somali Tea

MALAAK ABDALLAH

I am Somali
I am born with a love of tea
in the morning
in the evening
Somali tea, oh Somali tea.

For me and my family
it is more than tea
it is part of us, it is our culture,
tea is an addiction for me,
I cannot imagine
my life, even for a day, without Somali tea.

I make it sweet, add brown sugar
I open the cardamom pod and the fragrance dives
into the walls, tree-like, pungent and sweet,
I make the steaming water soak up the sugar
brew the tea leaves, steeping into my sweet tea.

I make it with love, I make it with love
I make it with hope
that I can brew my tea in Mogadishu
with a wood fire.
I make it with hope,
that I will make my tea in the sunset
of my motherland,

I will make my tea with love,
I will make my tea for all the people I love.

 For Malaak's recipe for Somali Tea, see page 143.

Ethiopian Coffee

ABDULREHIM SHUBA

Coffee, sweet lover
I've met you at last
how did I not discover you?
When I start drinking you, Ethiopian Coffee,
I will have you with a snack in the afternoon.
So, Coffee, never leave me,
Coffee, you must stay.

Home for the weekend
I opened a bag of fresh ground
Ethiopian *yirgacheffe* coffee,
it smelled like chocolate,
and like the earth of my country,
showing off new ways
to my old parents, to delight them
with the coffee of our country
to bring happiness to my father
and to my mother's back,
my mother, who stood at the stove.

In Ethiopia we also have Jimma Coffee
Jimma, city of coffee,
my Jimma forgotten, I smiled
and felt the memories of childhood
at my mother's stove.

For Abdulrehim's recipe for Doro wet, see page 122.

Lemons

NAINA RAI

Lemons remind me of Nepal
when I was in Nepal, I used to eat lemon slices,
people used to sell them on the street
each cost 10-15 rupees.

In Pancha 'Oti, the English School
waiting for the lunch bell to ring
we rushed out from the class
and ran all the way home, stopped
half way in the small market to buy lemons,
we were excited to carve them into little slices
of sunshine, eat them with salt, feel fresh,
laugh and go back to school.

When I was new in the USA
I used to eat lemons with salt
it reminded me of my friends, Lydia, Susma
and Anjana, I used to eat lemons with them
we would pinch our eyes and laugh
we put would them in chatpata.

No matter what, I just love to eat lemons.

Rice

Ebenezer Lian

Rice, looks short
feels warm and sticky
like the summers in Burma.
Mom would say *it's really good,*
Ben says *the best food ever,*
when I eat rice, I picture my family
coming home from work and from school.

Rice brings our family together
every time I devour rice
I remember back to Burma.

First you measure how much rice you want
then rinse it gently with cool water
next put it in a rice cooker.
After it's done cooking
it transforms from hard to fluffy,
the inside of the cooker looks like you're in heaven.

Rice, you are the only thing
that can bring our family together,
if you were not living with us,
my world would be nothing.

Ah rice, I don't want you
to just sit down at the table,
I don't want just to eat you and be content,
I want to walk into your fields
where the water is shining,
I want to stand there with you
far from the white tablecloth,
I want to fill my hands with the mud
of your fields, like a blessing.

Rice

RAM ZA THANG

When my mom taught me
how to cook rice
I was twelve,
she told me to wash the rice a couple of times,
rinse the rice really well,
until the water is clear,
then put it on the rice cooker.

Rice, short warm and fresh
sticky when you open
the rice cooker,
my dad would say
it is the best food in the world,
we ate it every day.
Ebennezer said it too,
rice is the best food in the world
because it is our culture's food,
in our culture we always eat rice
and vegetable, and egg, and meat,
if there is a wedding they would cook rice
and meat and soup.
We need to keep our culture
for the future, so we stick together
like sticky rice.

Cucumber

James Mung

Our biggest cucumber
is light green,
still covered in spikes,
young and defensive
like a teenager,

Mom wants me
to share it
saying it's better than
keeping it to myself
like a secret,

Dad says green cucumber
tastes lovely,
covered in chili salt,
I should have eaten more
food from my garden
before I came to the US,

I respect you, cucumber
still I poke you with my favorite fork,
my parents smile
laughing at the way
I devour my cucumber,
like a hunter shooting an arrow,

Peeling the hard green skin
is like sweeping the trash
in order to clear it out
to reveal the sweet soft seeds inside,
like reaching a dream.

Goodbye to you, cucumber of my country
I am leaving you to find
another garden that will have inferior soil,
I will remember that sunset
over you, garden of my country
like two halves of a once whole heart.

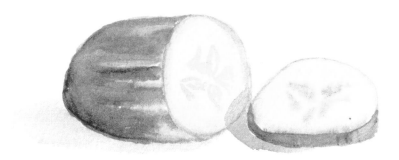

Lemon

RAM ZA THANG

The lemon tree in my parents' garden, in Burma
held in its branches bright lemons.
The lemons fell from the tree
with no apologies
for disconnecting themselves,
some of them laid on the ground rotting.

When I ate a lemon
my poor eyes watered.
My two cheeks quivered
and sucked in tight,
then my mother gave me
a cup of water with sugar in it.
I drank it in less than a minute.

Today, the smell of fresh lemons
reminds me of my parents' garden in Burma
because the lemons
always grew in that garden,
the branches swirled
and the lemons fell from the tree.
I still remember the heavy scent of lemon
that fell down when we cut the trees.

Arrival in a New Country: New Tastes

Where Food is an Art

NATHALY ROSAS

I am from a place where
The food is an art and every bite
Is a spicy piece of our culture
Where the smells call you to enjoy
And the flavors take you to your memories.

I am from where the trees grew up everywhere
*Guayabo, naranjo, alamos, manzano and palmera**
And the children take the special gift from them
Naranjas y limas, limas and limones †
Where the grocery stores have fresh items
Epazote, elotes, manzanas, melones y granada ‡
And bring us an exquisite dinner
Kneading and rolling, combination of flavors
Flavors that our indigenous ancestors gave us
Combination of oils and onions, always mixed
Picante y salado § gather and dance together.

Our food is not only food
It's a way to communicate our feelings
It's a way to talk with our family
It's our history, our identity.
But now everything is not the same
The tortillas smell different, the salsa is not spicy
Our special gifts are mixed with chemicals
Our food enclosed in a plastic prison.

Gradually, we will lose the essence, even in our own countries
The hands of our grandparents and our people were killed
The food of my family was thrown into the garbage
The cookbook of my grandmother was burned.

There is still hope
The gentle hands of my mother
Every day serving food.
Our kitchen table may be in another country
And the people who ate with us
Are no longer here,
But we will return to gather
In the morning lights
And the darkness nights
At the strong sound of the rain,
My aunties give this wisdom to my cousins
My parents give it to my brother and me
To conserve our special secrets.

* *Fruit trees*
† *A pun in Mexico*
‡ *Epazote, corn,apples, melon and pomegranate*
§ *Spicy and salty*

Donde la Comida es un Arte

Nathaly Rosas

Soy de un lugar donde
La comida es un arte y cada mordida
a Es una pieza picante de nuestra cultur
Donde los olores te llaman a disfrutar
Y los savores te llevan a tus memorias

Soy de donde los árboles crecen donde sea
Guayabo, Naranjo, Alamos, Manzano y Palmera
Y los ninos agarran los regalos especiales de ahi
Naranjas y Limas, Limas y Limones
Donde los mercados tienen cosas frescas
Epazote, Elote, Manzana, Melón y Granada
Y nos brindan una exquisita cena
Amasando y enrollando, combinación
de sabor
Sabores que nuestros ancestros indígenas dan
Combinación de aceites cebollas siempre
Picante y salado se juntan y juntos bailan

Nuestra comida no es solo comida
Es un modo de comunicar nuestros sentimientos
Es un modo de hablar con nuestra familia
Es nuestra historia, nuestra identidad
Pero ahora todo no es lo mismo
Las tortillas huelen diferente, la salsa no pica
Nuestros regalos especiales combinados con químicos
Nuestra comida encerrada en una prisión plástica

Perdemos la esencia inclusive en nuestros países
Las manos de abuelos y gente fueron muertas
La comida de mi familia tirada a la basura
El libro de la abuela ha sido quemado

Todavia hay esperanza
Las manos de mi madre
Cada día sirviendo comida
Nuestra mesa estara en otro país
Y nuestra gente quienes comían con nosotros
Ya no estan aqui mas
Pero volveremos a juntarnos
En la luz de la mañana
Y las oscuras noches
En el fuerte sonido de las tormentas
Mis tias dando sabiduría a mis primas
Mis parientes dandomelo a mi hermano y a mi
Para conservar nuestros secretos especiales

 For Nathaly's recipe for Mexican Quesadillas, see page 132.

Food: America/Iraq

Madyan Bakr

My story starts in 2014
when I first came to America
and left my home in Iraq.

In Iraq, we used to buy the animals
from an old man called Salih
and slaughter and cook them.
In America, we just buy them
from someone we don't know,
wearing some name tag
ready from the shop.

In Iraq, we used to eat meat with *Nan,*
we didn't need a fork; we used a spoon for rice.
Americans eat meat with spoons and forks,
not even touching the meat after they cook it.

In Iraq, we used to eat *Nan* with our food,
a long, circular shaped homemade bread,
using it to scoop up savory sauces, yogurts and meats.
In America, they make sandwiches.
I tried a sandwich once
with cheese and vegetables,
it was sticky, soft, disgusting,
I couldn't finish it and it made me sick,
I coughed and I said to myself,
I will not eat a sandwich anymore.

For Madyan's recipe for Doulmh (Iraqi Stuffed Grape Leaves), see page 117.

The New Pizza

Smile Khai

The first everything, in America
normal for them, new to me,
going to school with different uniforms
different everything, new everything,
the first day of school in America,
not knowing students raise their hand for an answer,
I raise my hand with confusion
wondering, why the bell rings so many times,
why I have more than one class,
why the teacher is so nice to the students?

RING RING RING! The bell has rung again
I followed my classmates; it was lunch time,
I looked around, I saw people getting their food,
I went to the line, *"hey!"* One of the teachers yelled at me,
I was so scared, I didn't know what to do,
thankfully, she pointed to where students were in line.

Finally, it was my turn, so I walked in, to get my food
there were three different foods, the first one
I couldn't see because it was packed into plastic,
the second looked like a bread, but with white cream on top,
the third one, it looked like a brain,
so I took the second food.

I picked up my food, it was hot!
I was confused: *I never saw a hot bread,*
I took one bite, I froze!
I gagged, I wanted to spit it out
but I saw the lunch teacher looking at me,
You don't like the food? We made it, and you don't like it?
so I swallowed slowly, I cried inside, deeply,
not because of the food, but because in that moment
I did not want to be in America,
I wished I could just fly back to my country
and eat *"laphet tuk."*

Laphet (also lahpet, letpet or leppet) is Burmese for fermented or pickled tea. Burma is one of very few countries where tea is eaten as well as drunk. Its pickled tea is unique in the region, and is not only regarded as the national delicacy but plays a significant role in Burmese society. Its place in the cuisine of Myanmar is reflected by the following popular expression: "Of all the fruit, the mango's the best; of all the meat, the pork's the best; and of all the leaves, lahpet's the best." In the West, laphet is most commonly encountered in tea leaf salad. (Wikipedia)

My Country's Cultural Food: Laphet

AUNG AUNG

When I arrived in U.S.A
I went to a restaurant with my uncle
I couldn't speak English very well
and I struggled to understand.
My uncle asked me, what I wanted
I didn't know what American food was,
I couldn't tell him
so, he ordered for me
the waiter brought a triangle
with chili, and melted cheese dripping,
I was so surprised
What is this?
He told me
It's called pizza,
never heard of this kind of food
never saw it before.

In my homeland, Burma
I never knew cowboy food.
In my homeland,
the most famous food
Is *Laphet*
green tea leaves,
sesame seeds,
fried peas,
dried shrimp,
fried garlic,
peanuts.

In America,
the school provided
breakfast and lunch,

bacon
eggs
biscuits
chocolate milk
milk
orange juice
apple juice

If we take those
we type our code number
on computer,
it was all new to me
and I was already full,
some of my friends giggled at me.

The stores in America
and the stores in Burma
are very different.

In my homeland,
we can't use enough refrigerators
because the store owner cannot afford them,
if we want to buy meat
early in the morning, they kill it for us,
the pig, chicken, or cow,
we take it home
devour it all in one day,
this is eating locally, organically,
this is what I came from.

See page 55 for a note on laphet.
For Aung Aung's recipe for Mohinga
(Burmese Fish Noodle Soup), see page 138.

Disapprovingly

James Mung

In Burma
growing up
we didn't use forks or spoons,
before eating,
my dad, Zua Pa, washed our hands
with love and care,
we waited for them to dry,
in order to devour our food with our hands
white rice, giving us energy.

In Tukwila,
when I tried to devour my food
with my hands
that I washed myself,
Americans stared at me
disapprovingly
in the school cafeteria.

At home though,
I still use my hands
it is our family's culture,
laughing, not feeling embarrassed.

El Salvador

Jennifer Escobar

In flavor or smell
the difference between food made with love
and food made too fast
is that it does not smell or feel
savory and rich
like in my country, El Salvador.

Here, the kitchen has no scent of recently made tortillas,
the tortillas have not just been made
between two loving hands,
but in a factory, stored away
in plastic bags, made many days ago.

Instead, you must plant the corn seed,
cook the corn, grind the corn in the mill
and then turn the pan with sticks,
only after doing it this way, you can begin to eat
echar tortillas en el comal.

In My Country

ABDULREHIM SHUBA

Here in America, there are
wonders everywhere
here the weather
could change at any time
in Adama, Ethiopia
it is moderate all of the time.

Here coffee is made
by a machine, too fast,
in my country
it is boiled on charcoal,
it takes its time.

Here sheep come
in plastic bags,
in my country,
they live with us.

Here grains and wheat
are washed by chemicals,
in my country the grains are fresh,
we wash them by our hands.

Here foods are eaten with spoons
but in Ethiopia we need
only our fingers and each other.

For Abdulrehim's recipe for Doro wet, see page 122.

Neighbors

ZAKARIA KAHIN

In my apartment
in Tukwila
I smell my cousin cooking
chicken with chili and garlic,
when I walk into the house
it smells of my country,
Somalia.

I hear
the stirring
of the bowl of oil
soft and special
like a soccer ball.

I hear my cousins
older than me
speaking in my language
talking about soccer games
and who won the latest match.

Outside of my apartment
in Tukwila
I smell the food my neighbors are cooking,
immigrants from other countries
I smell spicy food from many cultures—
Burmese, Mexican, Somali, and American food
mix together in the air,
I compare the smells of their food
to all the other cultures
a mixture of pancakes and syrup
blending with incense and halal meat.

I hear the chopping, frying
and sizzling sound
of other countries' foods,
when I walk through my apartment
I hear the music of their foods
when they cook.

A New Life

MAHENDRA BISWA

The international Airport in California
was our entry point
to our new lives in our new country,
we were surprised to see an Indian man
who did not talk to us
who did not know us
bring us delectable fried rice
on a plastic plate
that seemed to hold my life.

When I ate the fried rice I felt like
I was falling in love with America
and I didn't care what the world said,
or what some people who do not want to leave
Nepal say, that if we come to America we will suffer.
The fried rice was like an angel, like my sweet flawless life
as I was eating it, suddenly I wasn't in this world,
my mind was in another world
a world that gave me hope that I could return
to my country and help poor people.

In our country, Nepal, sometimes there are bad people,
from big cities who come to our refugee camp
and they want to steal our hope.
They want everything—land, houses, and even our young
women, who they say they will protect, but instead
they put them in danger's way.

But now in America I have found my hope
simply with a welcoming plate of fried rice,
the taste of my homeland.

For Mahendra's recipe for Paleu (Nepalese Rice Pudding), see page 146.

I Don't Like You, but I Like You the Most

By Zung Tin Mawi

My first month in Malaysia
I hung out with my friends Chin, Maw Hoi and Ni Sui.
We went to the restaurant
to have lunch,
the restaurant was full
with steaming bowls
of different kinds of noodle soup,
the smell was familiar, like Burmese *Mohinga*,
with noodles, deep curry, bright onion,
ginger and garlic.
I thought I would love to eat
Malaysian noodle soup,
but, when I ate it for the first time,
the sour, hot, spicy taste
wrinkled up my face,
I did not like the taste,
I did not like the Malaysian soup,
for the first year I did not like it.
But, after a year because my friends
always ate the soup,
little by little, I came to love Malaysian soup.

My Food from Guatemala

By Cindy Duarte-Reynosa

When I was in Guatemala
I saw how people planted tall trees
And how my family cooked every day
Rellenitos, garnachas, tamales, carne guisada
All the ingredients were natural.

When I came to the USA
The food was different,
Not fresh, not from the garden
But the food came with chemicals.

My culture's food is telling me
To relish her exquisite flavor
And remember that I have to be proud
Of my culture's fragrance and scents.

I hope one day I will
Eat my yellow *rellenitos*
When I go visiting
My Guatemala again.

I ate the food in my country
When we went to the carnival
There were many rides and games
And also traditional food—*garnachas* with women making them,
It was the best street food I know,
Now in the USA my mother and I
Can make the *garnachas*
But they are not the same
As the food of my Guatemala,
My home.

First Breakfast in America

ARUN BISWAKARMA

When I came from Nepal
I landed in California
the airport was shiny and impossibly clean,
my first breakfast was in that airport.
My case manager brought some food
on a black plate and sat next to me,
I ate fried rice with chow mein,
I drank a bottle of water
and ate spicy chicken.

I devoured the rice
sweet and spicy,
but I hesitated at the chicken
dyed a deep mysterious red.

Now when I see this food
I remember that day
when my family felt hungry,
when my family felt nervous,
but excited to eat this new food.

Tacos Son Vida

Roberto Diaz

Dear America,
I'm writing to let you know
you are doing tacos all wrong!!!
You don't make them with love.
Your tortillas are all stiff like an old *Mexican* man
who can't express joy,
your tacos don't have the same *sabor*,
yours are missing
chile hecho en comal,
cebolla cosida, salsa
echa en malcajeten y guacamole
hecho en molcagete.
The vegetables
the lettuce,
the tomato,
the onions,
the *aguacate*
are *rattone*
and your salsa, all speak
of a life in cans
and plastic packages,
not a life of fresh *fruteria* and love.

America, you need to know
that tacos are the tradition of all *Mexico*,
we can eat tacos for breakfast, lunch and dinner,
we share our homemade tacos with our neighbors
because they're part of the family.

Dear America, you should know
you are copying our cultural food
and that offends me,
because I don't think you know
how to make our food with love
like all Mexicanos make it.
Please, don't try to conquer the taco.

For Roberto's recipe for Arroz con Leche, see page 130.

Hi! America

VU NGUYEN

So cold, but I can brave
an American restaurant,
Cheesecake Factory,
look at menu
garlic pasta and shrimp?
don't know? try it!

Five minutes later
a hot dish of pasta
black of mushroom
yellow of pasta
and white of garlic sauce,
put some cheese on
cover the dish with the cheese
ready for it.

Hmm! the steam coming up
on this Tuesday, new in America,
use the fork and the spoon
to pick pasta up.

Wow! Unbelievable
in my head only one word
vai~!!!
I never ate something like this—
salt, coming from the sauce
and so much melting cheese
it's making my day
at this first time in my life.

13 Stripes and 50 Stars Coffee

KUM THAWNG HNIN

First day in America
coffee greets me
it's so bitter I need sugar
for sweetness, to remind me of the tea
in my homeland, Burma,
but I was new, so that day I mistook
white and creamy cheese
for sweet, creamy sugar
putting cheese into my coffee
with a small spoon
I sampled the coffee
and it remained bitter
so I poured it into the sink.

I vowed never to drink
the 13 stripes and 50 stars coffee
ever again,
but coffee still waited for me
to love it.

One day I went to school,
home of the Bulldogs
where my English teacher
who jokes about landing
in *Grammar jail*, had coffee,
I smelled 13 stripes
and 50 stars coffee
I was like hmmmm … ……

Yes, Coffee, you smelled sweet
and I was wanting you
so I went back home
and made the coffee
but that day I did not mistake
white and creamy cheese
for sweet and creamy sugar
and now you have become my thirteen stripes
and fifty stars coffee!

For Kum's recipe for Hinjo (Burmese Chicken Soup), see page 135.

Saving A Fish

NINI KHAING

A year ago, my family friend Som
invited my entire family
to eat dinner together at her apartment.
The dish we would eat was called (ปลาเผา) Pla Pao.
Her family lived far away from Tukwila,
it took three hours to get to Forks,
a city named after a utensil.

Som loved American dishes,
she is half Thai and half American,
when my entire family arrived
everything seemed like a traditional American house,
where shoes are worn inside,
where fences keep neighbors out,
and where water can be had in wine glasses.

Five minutes later
a strange sound come from the quiet house,
I could hear the sound of a heavy knife
chopping at an innocent life.
I tried to hide and watch to see what Som's mom was doing,
she was killing the fish, next to her kitchen sink,
but the fish was still alive,
a little water remained in the sink,
the fish was running with his tiny tail
the fish was glancing at me, with his wistful eye
the fish was tired of moving, for two minutes
I thought he tried to tell me to save him.

But fish are not for saving,
they are for killing and cooking,
as soon as Som's mom finished beating the fish
everybody was ready, to (รับประทานอาหาร) dine,
the fish smelled good to them
for me, the fish smelled bad.

On a beautifully flowered patterned plate
I saw the wistful fish,
calling out to me,
so I went outside
with the shovel in my right hand,
the fish in my other hand,
I dug in the soil for three feet
I put the fish in,
and covered it with soil,
and I said goodbye.

 For Nini's recipe for Thai Shrimp Fried Rice, see page 124.

Too Far from Home

Wilbert Alexander Anaya Murcia

In a small Vietnamese restaurant
where at night
the place is illuminated
with charming lights
and with a damp smell
because of the rain
combined with a new aroma
that ran to me from the kitchen
calling me to enjoy the food.

When I took my first bite of teriyaki
I was skeptical,
the moon shaped rice
and the sauce covered chicken
were different from my country,
this rice was bright white
with no spices on it,
Palido y sin color
El Salvadorian rice turns red
when cooked with spices,
and tomatoes and green peppers.

When the waiter brought me
"chopsticks" I felt ridiculous
because I didn't know
how to use them,
I tried to enjoy the teriyaki
but it was too far from home.

For Wilbert's recipe for Pupusas, see page 134.

69

Three Countries Home

Kang Pu

In my life
I have called
three countries home,
Burma, where meat is fresh
from the forest
where the hunter focuses on his target
not for sport, but for survival.

Fruit, we only ate after
we pulled it gently from the tree,
the spots covering its flesh,
holding it together,
vegetables were from the garden
with the redness of the soil,
like before the sunset,

When mom came back
from the garden
before she arrived,
I knew she was on her way
as the winds called
the smells of basil (*Leemmui*)
and the strong smell of earth's spices
around my home.
I felt mom's love,
I put my worries
into her pocket
to rest my love
in her heart.

In my new city in Malaysia,
meat was not fresh
just pushed into refrigerators,
cooked, it was covered with sauce
but the blood still showed,
thick like syrup
so I recoiled,
I didn't know
how I could eat it,
it reminded me of war victims.

In my current city, in America,
the grocery stores
do not smell of meat,
fruits or vegetables.

Sometimes I compare
three countries' meals,
their different smells,
and I ask myself why
did I leave Burma so soon,
the freshness of my mother's garden,
the food, the people, the life?

But, for now, I have enough food
more than in my country,
and I respect and I am proud
that I am at home with different meals
from three countries,
and my love rests in all of the foods
of my three countries.

Food in Times of Hunger, Conflict & War

A Person With a Dream

MADYAN BAKR

On June 14, 2014 when I left Shingal
I went to Dohuk
then to Erbil
to Jordan
to Egypt
to New York
to Chicago
to Seattle.

Traveled through all these cities
running from the war
that was about to explode in Iraq.

Living in Tukwila makes me forget
what happened with me in my travels
to my new life,
finding new places,
friends, school, and language,
and foods that I haven't seen in my life.

Going to miss my Iraq friends: Feras, Pasha, and Zidane,
my school Balistan, and the feeling of my past life.
A person with a dream that leaves war behind him
living in peace with a future that has freedom
misses his country, but he is relieved
for leaving the place of war,
he has a broken heart
that still wants to live.

For Madyan's recipe for Doulmh (Iraqi Stuffed Grape Leaves), see page 117.

My Flowers of Popcorn

JULIANNA MOE

Popcorn
like white and gray clouds
like sadness
like a sound of rain and thunder.
like the happiness
of the white sunny sky.

Popcorn
growing in a bowl like
flowers blooming on the clouds,
my bowl of popcorn.

The sadness that I kept inside for so long
that no one knew
except the clouds.
The clouds cried when I cried.
What a lovely friend I have
in the cloud
when there is no one.

We laugh together,
we cry together,
we share our history of brokenness
we understand each other
when there is no one.

 For Julianna's recipe for Mohinga (Burmese Fish Noodle Soup), see page 140.

Song

SOLOMON DAM

Let me not remember the Burmese government
for they do not help people,
let me not think of the hungry people,
let me not remember
the garden with the vegetables
and fruit that the goats destroy.

Let me not think of the hungry people,
let me close my eyes and think of my family's garden,
let me remember the taste of *fu*
that my mother and grandma planted for me,
let me not think of the way my mom
and grandma worked in our garden.

Let me not hear that the government
took away my garden,
let me not see my grandma angry,
let me not see how the government
kicked my people like a soccer ball,
let me not see how the government
threw my people like a baseball,
let me remember the way
my sweet grandma treated me.

I might forgive the Burmese government,
I close my eyes and I can see better days,
but I cannot sleep
when I think of the hungry people.

I can see children are crying,
I can see some people don't have homes,
I close my eyes and imagine
how it will be good for Burma's future
if the government respects my people.
I close my eyes and dream of peace
for my people,
I close my eyes and think
can someone tell me how can I change
the hunger and the struggle?
I close my eyes and pray for my people.
I close my eyes and remember
when my family was gardening and planting vegetables.

My Family's Corn

AUNG AUNG

With beautiful green leaves
and yellow kernels
it makes me feel bold,
it smells of Burma, Chin State
and I want to swallow each kernel.

As I write this poem about corn
I realize how much my grandpa loved me
when we lived together in my own country,
I remember how he loved his garden
and took care of his corn.

Corn can move everywhere
wherever it's been
it wants to help people
it wants to give
enough food and energy.

One day we cooked a pot of corn
we ate, all the family together
we smiled, we showed love to each other
we kissed our grandpa on both of his cheeks.

In my homeland we were such a poor family
and we couldn't eat too much rice
because we could not afford it,
most people could eat nourishing food
while my family could not.
But we always used to eat our corn with salt,
the corn tasted deeply sweet
and it was sustaining
to our bodies and our mind!

For Aung Aung's recipe for Mohinga (Burmese Fish Noodle Soup), see page 138.

My Beautiful People

Smile Khai

Memories of my auntie cooking,
fresh air coming into the window,
birds are having a conversation on a tree
about their hunger,
when I look out the window
sunlight is up on the tree,
looking at my neighbors' houses
they look lonely under the light of sunshine.

I close my eyes
and I see Tedim again,
birds flying under the sunshine light
above the light green leaves,
shining and reflecting from the sunlight.

I feel like I'm flying
when fresh air comes through my face
but, when I look at my people
the houses are like broken sticks,
this is all because of the government,
they don't take
full responsibilities for us,
most of us live
with hunger,
most of us live
with broken hearts.

No Food

KUM THAWNG HNIN

I picture my grey village, Kyar Inn, Kalay, Burma

The grey of soil and grass

I breathe deep and deep

I smell sadness

The crying

The shouting for help

Because of no food

No food, and without food,

We are not given peace.

 For Kum's recipe for Hinjo (Burmese Chicken Soup), see page 135.

The Food of My Country

ABDIRAHMAN ABDI

When my mother cooks, it smells of Somalia,
with memories of tea pouring in a cup,
memories of splashing oil and sizzling meat,
I picture the blue skies like our Somali flag,
I picture the deep green forests with mangoes
that are not yet ripe.

Yet, I taste the struggle
that my family has gone through,
struggle of food rationing
and never enough to eat,
struggle for clothing
not enough to keep us warm,
struggle for houses, with leaking roofs,
at night in the rain, only plastic bags over the roof.

Then the Ifo* refugee camp, better housing
but still not enough food, and so strange to our taste,
a taste of bitterness, we were not used it,
or the food rationing,
until we all spoke honestly, especially my mother.

Then they let my mother cook, over a small fire,
she cooked our Somali food.

In America we still cook our Somali food,
it travels with us wherever we go,
it is the taste of home.

* The camps of Dadaab are surrounded by barren desert. The three camps—Dagahaley, Hagadera and Ifo, known collectively as the 'biggest refugee camp in the world'—were established 20 years ago to house up to 90,000 people escaping violence and civil war in Somalia. With no end to the conflict in sight, there are now more than 350,000 people crowded into the camps' perimeters, while the number of new arrivals is surging. (Wikipedia)

To Fear

NGA REH

You that is in my heart
When the time is wrong,
like lightning you appear.
What are you? Where are you?
Where have you come from?
Do you have family?
You seem new born, like a newly hatched egg,
I should take you in, I should teach
you right from wrong,
you need protection from the unknown
of the world, from struggling to keep your emotions
in balance, not sad about leaving a place you love,
not so happy that you go overboard,
the unknown should be known to you,
only when the words right
from wrong are spoken
I should raise you as my own.

Lost in the River

ABDIRAHMAN ABDI

I was thirteen, leading my goats, my calves
and my sheep into the Somali forest
to find food,
I was hungry
my big sister and my friend
were hungry too,
when we were in the forest
we found a river that was cold and fresh
so we decided to take the animals
to drink water
because they were thirsty.

We were sitting in peace
while the animals drank
my sister was watching them drink
I was getting hungrier
so I went looking for food,
I saw a mango tree
and it had four ripe mangoes,
me and my friend ran to the tree
we climbed it, we pulled the green mangoes
I got one, my sister got one,
but my friend got two.

It was not fair for us,
we were hungry and wanted to share
the last mango, my friend disagreed
with our idea, so we decided
to throw the last mango down the river
so we would not get into a fight,
the mango, the lost mango, into the river.

Justice On Her Head

(FOR AUNG SAN SUU KYI ON THE EVE OF BURMA'S FIRST DEMOCRATIC ELECTION, NOVEMBER 8, 2015)

KUM THAWNG HNIN

Near Rangoon
in Burma
a woman carries justice on her head.
After a year of city drought
when a hundred students risked death,
she could no longer carry justice on her head.
With sorrow, water from her eyes and hungry
she went a far distance,
but there was no justice for her people.
One day, she came back from far away
and she carried justice again,
jail dissuaded her, but it could not stop her,
still she carried justice on her head.
Now the election is waiting
she carries justice on her head
to cast her vote,
and she is carrying justice on her head.

My Grandpa's Black Tea

(IN HONOR OF MY COUNTRY BURMA, COLONIZED BY THE BRITISH AND JAPANESE, STILL AT WAR)
BY KUM THAWNG HNIN

My sister makes tea for my grandpa
he drinks it everyday
our Burmese tea, strong and rich.

Grandpa tells us about the days
when two guests came, the colonizers
Shinzo Abe and Elizabeth II
who brought their tea,
the British tea, sweet with milk,
the Japanese tea, roasted and bitter,
they drank with my grandpa
suddenly, they wanted to impose
their tea on my grandpa's tea,
so it was that my grandpa's tea was at war
with Shinzo Abe and Elizabeth II.

When my grandpa was on vacation
Elizabeth II claimed my grandpa's cup of tea
she owned it for many years,
Shinzo Abe said to my grandpa *let's work together*
and you will get back your tea
grandpa agreed,
together they fought Elizabeth II
who owned my grandpa's tea
and he did get it back,
but Shinzo Abe did not return the tea
to my grandpa, he played with my grandpa's tea
and he shared it with his people.

My grandpa was a lion, a lion, a fierce lion,
and attacked Shinzo Abe because he lied
and so he destroyed him.

In the end,
grandpa got his tea back
by himself and restored his pride,
Democracy and Justice, people shouted
from their tea cups.

Our Small Town

BY JULIANNA MOE

Our small town in Tlang Zar,
our big green garden
the size of an American football field
and mountains and farms with pigs,
cows, horses and sheep grazing the grass.

I remember waking up in the early morning
on Christmas with sleep still on my face,
roosters screaming
our dog barking and jumping on me
with all his strength to welcome me.
The sunrise was red like a rose,
the air smelled like fresh earth
from the farmer's fields nearby,

Our neighbors woke up and began their day
cooking food for our town,
white sweet soft *Pauk see*
with meat inside, yellow *mohinga* soup
and a thousand more dishes,
foods as colorful as a rainbow,
the smell of sweet garlic
circulating from the fire pits outside,
made me a thousand times hungry,
the smell of food went up to the sky
like dandelion seeds.

We celebrated with excitement,
our town people were laughing with happiness
dancing around while cooking,
singing Christmas songs out loud at night
going around the whole house,
eating *San puih* at 11:00 around the campfire.

It was cold and cloudy
on another December morning
when we got out from the plane,
from Malaysia to the USA,
I could see my own breath,
the sky looked so lonely,
we walked and saw
my grandpa and uncles,
we got inside the car
the place looked so unfamiliar.
I realized that my future was
changing from now on.

The days went slowly, like a snail
that takes a million years to reach its home,
the sky was dark and rainy,
lightning was striking.

Only a short time in the USA,
I heard someone screaming,
I heard the house being turned
upside down, my heart beat faster,
I heard crying, my heart screamed out loud,
my mind wandered,
but I couldn't make any noise
so I cried silently.

I remember waking up
on Christmas morning,
waking up with tears and sadness
slowly walking in the living room,
finding the table, chairs and lamps
were upside down.
I thought life wasn't fair at that time.
What would a ten year old know
of what's going on?
What would a ten year old know
of sadness, loneliness, depression?

There was nothing to eat but hunger,
our family bond was broken like glass
that can't ever be fixed.
I hated this place more than anything else.
I felt like I was trapped in jail,
I felt like I was talking to the wall,
no one, there was no one who knew
how I felt, that was the day
my sadness turned to anger.

For Julianna's recipe for Mohinga (Burmese Fish Noodle Soup), see page 140.

Mother's Corn

KANG PU

Mother's corn
growing up in her garden,
quietly, it stayed underground
waiting for rain to raise it,
slowly it opened
its eyes and grew.

Corn could grow up too small
when it fought with rocks and winds
but every morning mom took care of it,
begged it for the future.
Corn, please! Please HELP me
and GROW! I am really sorry
if I neglected you
I was so humiliated,
I started to cry,
my tears washed all
the dust out of my eyes.

The government of Burma
wanted to steal the corn,
eat it themselves,
it made them proud
when they separated
the kernels from the cob,
like separating families
from each other.

My mom answered in
a trembling voice,
Why did you come here?
Return my family to me.
but they warned,
We will not let you be free
to stay here.

Mom sat alone by herself,
to think of all the kernels
my brothers and my sister,
her eyes were not laughing at all.

My brothers and my sister
from far away like
the kernels are crying together
wishing to get back home,
holding the cob strong,
the cob like my mom,
had laughing eyes,
the kernels held in her arms
she is saying to us
You are free
and I am still holding you,
no matter what our past.

In our memory,
Mom would now
be an old woman
she would open her eyes
and tell the kernels,
I remembered that time
we were separated
from the garden
it paralyzed my mind
after we parted
I was a lonely bird
that murmured late
in the night.

Now, my family has
no more tears,
laughing eyes again,
all tears are united
in love and empathy,
the corn gives more life again
the garden is full of peace
and no more hunger.

For Kang Pu's recipe for Zawngtah (Burmese Tree Beans with Tilapia), see page 136.

The Taste of War: Pomegranates

SMILE KHAI

The taste of a war
as if bitter and sweet are fighting,
the sounds of painful hearts
beating for help.

When I close my eyes
I can see my country and my people
at the same time and I can taste
the bitterness of war,
now my people are thirsty for water
hungry for food,
the government is weakening my people.

Now we have eyes that do not see us
and ears that will not hear us
that force us
every time when we try to escape,
everywhere is silence
everywhere is darkness
until the day comes
until the sweetness.

Finally, we can see the morning sunlight smiling
suddenly, I open my eyes
the painful tears that are left behind
are saying "goodbye" to each other
the war has ended.

I can taste the sweetness,
because it has finally won the war,
now the darkness of bitter is left behind
now we can finally smile with sadness,
the bitter and the sweet.
the red of the blood,
like the color of the pomegranate,
has gone away.

My Home Before the War

Madyan Bakr

The color of the sky in Kurdistan, blue,
my friends laughing, smiling and playing
when we played soccer,
the feeling of the people walking in the village
and the feeling when they were sad,
they still tried to laugh.

The picture of my mom's kitchen
she is cooking rice, chicken and meat,
then, our family around the table,
I picture Kurdistan as it was in peace,
when we were there.

But now it is in war,
war that leaves us with no home
traveling through Jordan and Egypt,
just so we will not be killed by ISIS
leaving, yet hoping to see Iraq
in peace.

Remembering the Gardens, Cooking & Kitchens of Loved Ones

My Mother's Kitchen

KANG PU

When my mom cooked it smelled of sweet wintertime cherries,
of a solitary forest with rain falling
and it smelled like the murmur of a lonely bird, singing.
I picture the spherical smoke rising from her kitchen
it was like the sound of sleep at night,
it was like arriving home safe and sound
the sounds of her kitchen were peaceful.

I still long for the laughter of those family meals
we all waited for that table, my mom's table,
how she prepared every family meal,
this is what I still long for,
so often I remember my mother
nothing can take her memory away from me,
it is truly difficult that I have departed
from my motherland,
and from my mother's kitchen.

For Kang Pu's recipe for Zawngtah (Burmese Tree Beans with Tilapia), see page 136.

My Grandmother's Garden

Zung Tin Mawi

When I close my eyes
I see my grandmother's house
that has a big back yard
and beautiful garden
inside her garden
it has fruit like
mango, papaya
and banana.

In the morning
when the sunshine came out,
the sun hit the garden
it made it more beautiful.

In the afternoon
there were many kinds
of animals' sounds
birds, dogs and hens.

When my grandmother cooked
delicious food from her garden
like *sabuti* and *moeheinkha*,
I felt like I was rich
when I went to her garden.

Calendar for Sabuti

CECILIA DAWT IANG

March is the time the farmer sows my seeds
April is the time my seeds sleep in the darkness and rain
May is the time I start to see the light
June is the time my seeds start to stand
    by themselves with beautiful life
July is the time I build family
August is the time I take care of the sweet baby
September is the time to open my husk
    and show my baby to the world,
    the color of my body—sunshine
    the taste of my body—sweet
October is the time I dry in the sun
    pounding in the mortar making me into soup
    they make it with salt
    chili pepper, lemon, and celery,
    I become the name of "Sabuti"
    not only for their family
    but sharing with the neighborhood and friends.
The day they cook Sabuti,
is the day they transform me
from the sun, rain and soil
to nourishing bowls of Sabuti.

Nepalese Kitchen

MAHENDRA BISWA

I picture in my country
how my mom is cooking vegetables,
I'm standing in the kitchen next to her
and watching how she cooks,
and I'm thinking about how can I help her
so she doesn't have to work so hard
every day in the kitchen,
she is tired and puts her hands on her head.

My mother's kitchen is the sound of classical music,
it is the taste of a beautiful red sky,
it is the colors of fall and of summer,
it is like sun in the morning time
when we eat our country's food,
Dal-bhat, tarkari with chutney,
traditional food that I love from my country,
from my mother's kitchen,
like her sweet rose cake.

 For Mahendra's recipe for Paleu (Nepalese Rice Pudding), see page 146.

My Grandmother's Mint

SAMA JABBARIMEHMANI

I remember my grandmother,
how she grew mint in her garden,

I remember it was medicine for my mind
when I smelled the mint in her garden,
I imagined a calm forest.

Yes, mint smells like a calm forest,
when I breathe mint
it makes my mouth feel cold and fresh.

My grandmother would make a drink of mint lemonade,
she mixed mint, lemons and water together in her blender,
this drink was wonderful medicine for my heart.

Mexican Kitchen/Cocina Mexicana

NATHALY ROSAS

Memories of the kitchen table
Memorias de la mesa de la cocina
Place where we gave thanks
Lugar donde dabamos gracias

The table filled with *La mesa llena con*
Tamales, tacos, picadas and tortillas

Place where parents give advice
Lugar donde parientes dan consejos
"Don't be selfish"
"No seas egoista"

"Don't be lazy"
"No seas flojo"

"Be respectful"
"Se respetuoso"

"Be helpful"
"Se ayudador"
"Be a worker"
"Se trabajador"

Where birthdays and Christmases pass
Donde cumpleanos y Navidad pasan

I taste our dreams in the air
Pruebo nuestros sueños en el aire

At this table
En esta mesa
Forever together
Por siempre juntos
At this table
En esta mesa
Words like "Get off the table"
Palabras como "Bajense de la mesa"
At this table
En esta mesa
My memories forever
Mis memorias por siempre

 For Nathaly's recipe for Mexican Quesadillas, see page 132.

My Family in My Mother's Kitchen

JAMES MUNG

When my mom cooks, it smells of sweet cooking oil,
there is the sound of stirring a big pot,
the sound of vegetables sizzling into bowls
and scents of beautiful oil, the color of sunflowers,
there is the waiting to taste her cooking,
there is the grinding of chili
and outside there are pigs rolling in the earth
chickens waiting
and the sweetness of snowy rice.

I picture our colorful house,
the brownness of the earth,
the wonder of the wind,
I can feel the strong, deep family tree,
our love is not just love.

Brother

Zakaria Kahin

This is Liban
our caring brother
who works to get money for us
for food
for clothes.

This is Liban
our caring brother
who every day thinks of us
and thinks of my grandma in Somalia,
every month he sends his paycheck
back to her in Somalia.

This is Liban
our caring brother
making us dinner,
for my three brothers
my one sister and my mom
making us Somali food—jabati, injera, and strong coffee

This is Liban
keeping our family
out of danger.

For My Grandmother—the Strongest Woman

MALAAK ABDALLAH

The strongest woman I have heard about
the woman who had no chance to go to school
the woman who never learned to write or read
but she had life knowledge and wisdom,

the woman who worked at age nine
the youngest girl in her family, she worked in the morning
selling eggs at Hamar Waane market
she worked at night,
selling cow's milk at the center of Wardhigaley.

The strongest woman I have heard about
the mother of six children and also the father at the same time,
the mother who struggled to raise five daughters and one son,
the strongest woman I have heard about
her main work, her income for raising her six offspring
was only by selling eggs,
she was the strongest woman I have heard about.

I am proud to tell out loud
that this strong woman, Madiina Abdi Miriq,
is my grandmother.

For Malaak's recipe for Somali Tea, see page 143.

Family Garden

SOLOMON DAM

My family had a big garden in Burma,
we had bananas, cucumbers, potatoes,
onions, garlic, pumpkins and lettuce,

My family loved the potatoes,
brown on the outside, inside white.
I miss our family meals,
I miss gardening together
with my cousins, my grandparents,
my aunties and uncles.

When I am old enough, I will return to them,
I will go back to the garden and work
with my grandparents,
I miss them, I want to taste
the food of our garden
with my family again.

My Mother's Kitchen

Jeewan Poudel

My mother's *kheer* is made of rice
it takes almost 90 minutes to make it
it sounds like lava flowing from a volcano
it tastes of bright sun.

My mother moves silently through the kitchen
in her quiet world,
I watch her move
like water through a river,
her pudding is scented with cardamom,
saffron, and cashew nuts,
it reminds me of my childhood
eating *kheer* back in my Nepal
with my family.

For Jeewan's recipe for Kheer, see page 144.

My Grandmother's Cooking

RODAS NEGUSSIE

When my grandmother cooks it smells of injera,
I remember when I was a little girl,
my grandma was always cooking for me
she took care of me,
I remember the morning food smells
making me hungry,
I remember the stories of my family tree
she told me before I went to sleep,
I remember her warm hugs,
I can still picture her telling me about the history
of my ancestors. I was blessed
to have my grandmother with her sunshine smile
and her cooking.

My Father's Cooking

Ebenezer Lian

When my father cooks, it smells of white rice,
I remember when my father cooked,
I saw the boiling water and went outside,
the sun was bright
and two sisters were playing,
I stood, watched and heard
birds singing in the trees with happiness,
there was the smell of fresh air,
I can picture my father's cooking
meat and rice, I can taste my father's cooking
and the joy in his food he gave
to my mother and the love.

Apples

Avnoor Brar

My shiny and red apple,
ripe for me and my family,
is ready to share its life.

Aman and Arnav take the seeds of my apple,
to grow in their garden,
to ripen another apple
again and again,
someday.

My friend Harjot,
scolds me,
apple trees
need special care
that you don't give,
I begged him, *please tell me,*
he said, *proper fertile soil,*
and water three times a day.

Apples struggle to grow
for me,
wind and rain force,
force them to the ground,
but the apple tree gave
more apples to me.

And now the apple smiles,
a red shiny face,
but when the apple sees the knife,
the apple cries,
it is smooth and rough inside
like skin in winter.

Apples from the Trees

AUNG AUNG

When my grandmother cooks
the kitchen smells of her serene voice
her voice comes from her heart,
she fed me when I was a child,
corn in her cooking pot.

I can still picture the community members
in my country, Burma, Chin State,
all the adults in a group talking
like the sounds of horns honking,
when I heard their loud voices
I was shouting.

But community elders are always teaching
their members
if the apple tree doesn't get enough water,
it cannot grow up,
like that, when you grow up you must not forget
your community members
they have told you,
Don't say bad words,
don't judge people by their appearance,
If you can help those who are in need
try to help them.

Ripe apples give us allegiance and dignity,
the best way
for every community member
and every leader.

Cooking Nepali Fish

SAGAR RAI

Memories of my country fill my heart,
I remember my country, Nepal,
I was ten years old
and I always went to the Sita Khola River
to catch fish,
and my mother always cooked them for me.

I loved her cooking of the rice
and her frying of the fresh fish
with oil, cabbage, and hot spicy red
and green peppers,
I remember the smell of frying oil
and the plate full of tiny fish.

I caught those fish,
my mother cooked them,
but only my brother and I ate them,
before my father came home in the dark,
we had eaten those fish.

My Grandmother's Garden

Julianna Moe

When my grandma cooks, it smells of chicken soup,
I remember waking up in Burma in the early morning,
and watching the sun rise from the red blood orange sky,
birds chirping, dogs barking,
seeing my grandfather standing
in front our house and just watching
the beautiful sky made me feel
like I was in a whole new world.

I picture my grandmother's big garden,
the green colors of cucumber, lettuce and peas
the fresh smell of the flowing water
the sound of bamboo trees
and the river,
the feeling of the cold
air weaving through my hair,
seeing the tall corn
with my sister laughing and playing
around the garden. I taste the happiness
that I will never taste again in my whole life.
These memories of my grandmother's garden,
I will never forget.

Emelina is My Grandmamy

Jennifer Escobar

Emelina is like a pomegranate
Sweet, bright red, deep of heart,
Inside of her heart, there is much love
Like the seeds of a pomegranate.

Emelina is like a pomegranate
With her big heart,
With her kindness,
With her wisdom,

That's my grandmother in El Salvador
With her sweet heart,
With too much love inside
Like the seeds of a pomegranate.
I miss her every day
I miss her cooking—*pupusas, tamales, atol,*
I miss her with all of my heart,
My grandmamy.

Fried Rice

Hai Nguyen

I was born in Vietnam,
When I was growing up,
I used to eat fried rice,
That my mother made.

Rice is white,
But when fried,
It looks golden.

When my mother cooked,
She always worked hard,
Cutting the tomato,
Mixing greens for the salad,
When the rice was ready,
My mother tried it,
I knew it was good
When she smiled.

Then I tried it,
I closed my eyes,
It smelled of hard work
And love from my mother,
And I said to her
Thank you for this food.

Fried rice is so lovely,
When I eat it,
It brings happiness
To my face.

Standing In My Grandmother's Garden

Cecilia Dawt Iang

It is raining and raining
and my grandmother's garden
is filled with strawberries,
peaches, apples, oranges,
carrots, potatoes,
tomatoes and chilies,
cucumbers, peas and garlic,
cabbage, celery and green beans.

All of her vegetables and fruits
taste as sweet as my parents' love.
When I stand in my grandmother's garden,
it feels like traveling the world.

My Father's Kitchen

MALAAK ABDALLAH

Memories of my father's cooking fill my head
when my father cooks it smells Yemeni
the fish Masala mixed with pepper
remind me of my father's kitchen.
Memories of his rice mixed with saffron
are like the morning sunrise.
The memories of splashes of oil
are like an ocean of honey,
the memories of sizzling fish
are like the sound of the warm wind.

I picture my father's hands
shining with the color of orange saffron,
I picture the steaming fish like heaven,
I picture the deep brown of the tamarind juice.

I can feel the love of my father's hands,
I feel his hard work,
the tenderness of his country Yemen
in my father's kitchen.

My Grandmother's Cooking

Helen Boih

When my mother and grandmother cook it smells of Burma,
sometimes at midnight I dream about my mother and grandmother
cooking fish and tomatoes mixed into a beautiful scent,
it sounds like my mother is telling me my future.

My memories of food are of my grandmother cooking,
though she is no longer here,
like a hard rain that never stops,
it's hard to say goodbye.

I remember my grandmother praying
for me and my siblings,
her food was not just food,
but beautiful, like precious gold
tasting of love and sunsets.

I picture the beautiful blue sky,
the deep color of my grandmother's heart,
I picture a smooth fruit, like my grandmother's prayers,
a soft wind weaves through my hair
when I remember the scents of my grandmother's cooking.

Recipes

Foods from Our Homelands

"I had to wait for five minutes for it to cool down enough to eat. Those five minutes were painful! I could never wait."

Doulmh: Iraqi Stuffed Grape Leaves

MADYAN BAKR, IRAQ

When my mom makes Doulmh, it reminds me of my village in Iraq when I ate it with my friends. I could always smell the warm rice and grape leaves when it was done cooking, but I had to wait for five minutes for it to cool down enough to eat. Those five minutes were painful! I could never wait.

MAKES ENOUGH FOR 6 TO 10 PEOPLE TO ENJOY

Ingredients:

- 3 cups of cooked rice
- 3-4 potatoes
- 4 tomatoes
- 1 large white onion
- 30-40 grape leaves
- ½ tablespoon cumin
- 3 tablespoon of olive oil
- 1-2 tablespoons of salt
- ½ cup lemon juice
- 1½ cups of water
- 2 tablespoons tomatoes paste

Method

1. First get everything ready. Wash or clean the rice, potatoes, tomatoes, onions, and grape leaves.

2. Then mix the rice, tomato paste, cumin, and oil.

3. Then put the grape leaves on the table. Place a tablespoon of the rice mixture on the grapes leaves and fold the sides of the leaves in and roll it like cigar. Place the rolled leaves in a large pot for cooking.

4. Then add the tomatoes and onions to the pot.

5. Add lemon juice and water in stock pot and cook it on the stove for 1½ hours on low heat.

Sholeh Zard: Iranian Saffron Rice Pudding

SAMA JABBARIMEHMANI, IRAN

In Iran we eat this dish for holidays, but my family and I enjoy eating this in the mornings with cinnamon powder. I remember when my mom made this dish, the smell of saffron filled the room and clung to my hair.

FOR 4 PEOPLE

Ingredients:

- 1 ½ cups white rice
- 8 cups water
- 1 cup white sugar
- ¼ canola oil
- ⅓ cup rose water
- 2 teaspoons powdered saffron
- 2 Tablespoons blanched slivered almonds
- 2 Tablespoons ground pistachios
- 1 Tablespoon ground cinnamon

Directions/Method

1. Wash rice. Rinse and drain the rice several times until the water runs clear. Add the rice to a large, heavy bottomed saucepan.

2. Add 8 cups of water to the pot and partially cover with a lid. Bring the rice to a boil over medium heat, occasionally skimming the foam off the top.

3. Put saffron into 2 teaspoons of warm water and set aside.

4. Once rice is soft and boiling (approximately 30 minutes), add sugar and stir gently to dissolve. Add an additional 2 cups of water and stir to combine. Keep the rice partially covered and continue to cook over a medium low heat for approximately 20 more minutes. Stirring occasionally.

5. Put canola oil, rose water and the ground saffron threads along with their water into the rice and stir thoroughly to combine. Continue to cook, partially covered, for another 20 minutes over low

heat.

6. Remove the lid and stir well. The mixture should start to look like a thick pudding, like cream; all the water should be boiled out at this point. Feel free to add more saffron to taste. The more saffron you add the richer the flavor and color of the pudding.

7. Add the blanched slivered almonds and continue cooking over medium low heat until a pudding-like texture develops (approximately 30 more minutes).

8. Once thickened, remove the pot from the stove and pour the Sholeh Zard into a large, shallow plate and let it cool. Once the top has dried into a thin, yet hard, layer you can decorate with the cinnamon and pistachios in a pretty pattern. You can make simple patterns or ones that are very complex. For examples of how this traditional pudding is decorated see: google images for Sholeh Zard—it's amazing food art!

9. Once cool, place the plate, covered into the refrigerator and continue chilling until the pudding has transformed into a jello-like consistency.

10. Optional serving styles: The pudding also tastes great warm (right after it's done cooking).

11. Whichever way you choose, we like both. You may now serve the tastiest dessert along with a nice cup of tea

"The smell of saffron filled the room and clung to my hair."

Doro wet: an Ethiopian Chicken Stew

RODAS NEGUSSIE, ETHIOPIA

This is a favorite traditional Ethiopian dish that my aunts made for me. In my country there are many different ways to spice and prepare this dish.

Ingredients:

- ¼ cup lemon juice
- 2 Tablespoons salt, plus more as needed
- 4 bone in chicken thighs
- 3 cups chopped onions
- 3 garlic cloves, minced
- 1 Tablespoon peeled, minced fresh ginger (½ inch piece)
- water (optional)
- ¼ cup butter
- 2 Tablespoons paprika
- 1 cup berbere paste*
- ¾ cup chicken stock
- 1 teaspoon cayenne pepper, or to taste
- freshly ground black pepper
- 4 hardboiled eggs, peeled
- Injera an Ethiopian bread or hot cooked rice to serve

Directions/ Method:

1. Combine the lemon juice and salt in a large, nonreactive mixing bowl and stir until slightly dissolved.

2. Add the chicken thighs, one at a time, dipping both sides of each piece in the marinade to coat. Cover and allow to marinate in the refrigerator for about 30 minutes.

3. While the chicken is marinating puree the onions, garlic and ginger in a food processor or blender. Add a little water if necessary, to get the blades moving.

4. Heat the butter in a Dutch oven over medium heat and stir in the paprika to color the oil.

5. Stir in the berbere paste and cook for 3 minutes, until heated through.

6. Add the onion mixture and sauté until most of the moisture evaporates and the mixture is reduced, about 15 minutes. Add cayenne to taste and season with salt and pepper.

7. Remove the chicken from the lemon juice and discard the marinade. Add the chicken to the pot and cover with sauce. Bring the sauce to a boil, reduce the heat to low, cover and simmer for 45 minutes, flipping the chicken halfway through. Add water, if necessary, to maintain the liquid level.

8. Add the whole hard boiled eggs and continue to cook until the chicken is very tender, 10 to 15 minutes. Adjust seasonings and serve hot with injera bread or rice.

*Berbere *supplies one of the unique flavors of Ethiopian cuisine. There really is no substitute. Use as many of the spices as you can, but do try to use fenugreek and the dried peppers or paprika. They supply an essential flavor. You can find a recipe for this paste with its many spices if you go to "berbere paste" on google where it will tell you that, "Berberē is a spice mixture whose constituent elements usually include chili peppers, garlic, ginger, basil, korarima, rue, ajwain or radhuni, nigella, and fenugreek. It serves as a key ingredient in the cuisines of Ethiopia. Although the American cook can find berbere in specialty stores, it sometimes encompasses herbs and spices that are less well known and not available outside of Ethiopia; this includes both cultivated plants and those that grow wild in Ethiopia." (Wikipedia & internet recipe sites)*

Doro wet: A Variation of Ethiopian Chicken Stew with Optional Niter Kibbeh*

ABDULRAHIM SHUBA, ETHIOPIA

In my family, we eat this dish on Eid, a Muslim holiday. My grandma always prepared this dish for us in Itaya, Ethiopia. I remember when she cooked this dish for us, and the powerful scent of the stew. Many people in our culture enjoy eating this popular dish for lunch. It is best to cook this dish with the drumsticks of the chicken. You should remember to cook this slowly, so the ingredients have a half of a day to blend in together.

THIS RECIPE SERVES SIX PEOPLE.

Ingredients:

- 1 large package of chicken legs and thighs, skinless
- 3 lemons, juice only
- 2 teaspoons salt
- 4 lb onions, chopped
- 3 cloves garlic, crushed
- 1 Tablespoon ginger root, peeled and chopped
- 1 cup oil, butter or niter kibbeh*
- 1 cup berbere paste
- 1 cup water or chicken stock
- 6 hard-boiled eggs (optional)

Directions/Method:

1. Mix together the chicken pieces, lemon juice and salt in a large non reactive bowl and set aside to marinate for about 30 min

2. While the chicken is marinating, puree the onions, garlic and ginger in a food processor or blender. Add a little water if necessary

3. Heat the oil, butter or niter kibbeh in a clay pot over medium flame. Add the paprika and stir into color the oil and cook the spice through, about 1 min. Do not burn, stir in the berbere paste and cook for another 2 to 3 min.

4. Add the onion garlic-ginger puree and sauté until most of the moisture evaporates and the onion cooks down and loses its raw aroma, about 5 to 10 min. Do not allow the mixture to burn.

5. Pour in the water or stock and stir in the chicken pieces, cayenne to taste, salt and pepper. Bring to a boil reduce heat to low, cover and simmer for 45 min. Add water as necessary to maintain a sauce- like consistency

6. Add the whole hard boiled eggs and continue to cook for another 10 to 15 minutes, or until the chicken is cooked through and very tender

7. Adjust seasoning and serve hot with injera bread or rice.

*Niter Kibbeh, *like berbere powder or paste, is basic to the wonderful flavors of Ethiopian cooking; it tastes great on many things: steamed vegetables, mashed potatoes, and steamed rice. It can be used to add extra flavor to many fried foods, and you can find recipes for it on-line. The basic ingredients for a batch that will last through several dishes are: unsalted butter, chopped red onion, chopped garlic, chopped ginger root, 1 1/2 teaspoon turmeric, green cardamom pod, whole cloves and fresh ground nutmeg. (Wikipedia)*

Recipe for (ข้าวผัดกุ้ง): Thai Shrimp Fried Rice

NINI KHAING, THAILAND

When I came home from school in Thailand, I could smell the scents of my mom's Shrimp Fried Rice coming right through the air and covering my face. We took the vegetables from our garden and the shrimp came right from the nearby sea; we didn't have to pay for anything. I only ate this dish on school days. This is a simple food that my mom made. I always sat on our deck with a lovely view of the ocean and ate my Shrimp Fried Rice. Shrimp Fried Rice, I'll never forget you.

MAKES 2 SERVINGS, AS A GOOD SNACK, OR LIGHT MEAL

Ingredients:

- 10 shrimp peeled and deveined
- 2 cups of cooked day-old rice
- 1 cup of fresh snow peas
- 2 large fresh carrots, chopped
- 3 eggs
- Pinch of Kosher salt
- 2 Tablespoons of olive oil (1 each for the sauté and the wok)
- 1 ½ teaspoons of soy sauce
- 4 large garlic cloves, finely chopped
- 3 teaspoons white pepper powder

Directions/Method:

1. Steam the chopped carrots until tender, when tender remove them from the heat and set aside
2. In a medium saucepan heat1 T. olive oil high heat
3. Sauté garlic
4. Add shrimp and sauté
5. Add kosher salt
6. Add white pepper powder
7. In a large wok heat 1 T. of oil over high heat
8. Scramble the eggs
9. Add sautéed shrimp
10. Stir-fry 30 seconds to remove moisture
11. Add snow peas
12. Add steamed cooked carrots
13. Stir-fry 30 seconds to remove moisture
14. Add old rice
15. Continue to stir-fry
16. Add soy sauce

Thai Fish Chowder with Tomatoes and Lemongrass

THAN WIN, THAILAND

Back in Mae La refugee camp, when my friend's mom died, it was an unlovely and sad day. People were everywhere, and in a way, this very sad moment was like a party. There were many different kinds of foods brought by relatives and neighbors. The food seemed to make people feel better, to me the taste of this Thai fish chowder was a taste of happiness.

SERVES 6 TO 8 PEOPLE

Ingredients:

- 2 tablespoons chili powder
- 2 ¼ cups of fresh green peas
- 2 medium sized onions or 4 shallots, diced
- 5 cloves garlic
- 1 4-inch stalk lemongrass
- ½ tablespoon turmeric
- ½ tablespoon salt
- 5 tablespoons canola oil
- 2 Roma tomatoes, diced
- 3 large fillet of white fish, cut into 3-inch pieces
- Large handful fresh cilantro, coarsely chopped for the garnish

Directions/Method:

1. Using a food processor, pulse the chili powder, onions or shallots, garlic, turmeric, together to mince and combine.

2. Place a skillet, preferably nonstick, over medium high heat and add the oil. Sauté the onion-garlic mixture in the pan until the onions just start to turn translucent and the mixture sizzles and smells sweet.

3. Add the tomatoes and about a tablespoon of water to keep the mixture moist but not soupy. Cover and let simmer for about 10 minutes, stirring occasionally.

4. Add the fish, more salt to taste and enough water to cover the bottom of the pan. Cover and let simmer for about 15 minutes or until fish is flaky and cooked through.

5. Garnish with fresh cilantro and serve with rice.

"This Thai fish chowder
was a taste of happiness."

Com Chien: Vietnamese Fried Rice

Hai Nguyen, Vietnam

In my culture, we often eat this dish. My mother always prepared this dish for us in Vietnam. I remember the strong scent of spice and I can still hear her telling us stories of the dishes she cooked. I remember her showing me how to cook it. We enjoyed eating this food in the morning with milk, though many people in our culture enjoy eating this popular dish for dinner. It is best to cook this dish with only fresh ingredients from a nearby garden. This dish is best prepared with lots of love and happiness. You should remember to cook this slowly, so the ingredients have time to get to know one another.

Serves about four people

Ingredients:

- Four to Six cups cooked steamed rice, cooled completely, the grains separated, then chilled
- 1 tbsp peanut oil in wok
- ¼ cup light soy sauce
- 2 tsp. sesame oil
- 1 Tbsp. of sugar (optional, but often used)
- ¾ cup of fresh snow peas
- 1 carrot finely chopped
- 1 medium onion finely chopped
- 4 green onions finely chopped.
- ¾ cup of bean sprouts
- 2 eggs cooked and chopped

Method:

1. Combine soy sauce with sesame oil and optional sugar; set aside.

2. Heat peanut oil in the wok over high heat and add onion, when it begins to cook well, then add peas and carrots and -stir-fry for 3 minutes.

3. Add in optional meat, chicken or fish and continue to stir fry.

4. Add rice and then the soy sauce mixture and chopped egg to rice mixture and fold in; stir-fry for 1 minute more; then toss in bean sprouts.

5. You can add Char Siu (roasted pork), or a salad of spicy greens or tomato and serve in individual bowls.

"This dish is best prepared with lots of love and happiness.

You should remember to cook this slowly, so the ingredients have time to get to know one another."

Arroz Con Leche: Mexican Rice with Milk Pudding

Roberto Diaz, Mexico

My grandmother loves to cook Arroz Con Leche because it is one of the most traditional desserts of the cuisine of Mexico and Central American countries; but is a specialty of my city, Aguascalientes. Arroz Con Leche reminds me of how my grandmother's house was filled with the intense aroma of vanilla as she made this dessert. I remember when I helped my grandmother go to the store to buy the ingredients.

Ingredients

- 1 litro de leche.
- 110 gr. de arroz.
- 110 gr. de azúcar.
- 1 rama de vainilla.
- ½ rama de canela.
- Canela en polvo.
- 2 latas de lechera.

1 liter of milk.
110 grams of rice.
110 grams of sugar.
 1 vanilla pod.
½ cinnamon stick.
½ to 1 tsp. of powdered cinnamon.
2 cans of sweetened condensed milk.

Directions/Method

primero hajara una olla le pones 6 tasas de agua lo dejas en la estufa asta que llerva la agua y luego le pones 3 tasas de arroz dejas el arroz hasta que asuerba la agua el arroz y lo dejas en yama baja y luego le pones 3 tasas de leche lo degas en yama baja para que no se peje el arroz y luego le pones 2 rajitas de canela y 1 tasa de leche condensada y le pones 1 tasa de leche evaporada y le pones una 1 tasa de azucar me nele para que se mixtie los sabores y tambien meneale para que no se peje el arroz y lo meneas por 5 minutos y luego le pones 1 tasa llena de vainilla y para darle mas sabor le pudes poner 1 cuchardita de limon verde rallada y tambien le pones 1 tasa de coco rallado

First boil 6 cups of water in a pot. Once it boils, add 3 cups of rice and cook until it has absorbed all the water, then lower the flame. Add three cups of milk, keeping the flame low so the rice doesn't stick, and then add the powdered cinnamon and cinnamon stick broken in half and 1 cup of condensed milk, and then add the additional cup of condensed milk and 1 cup of sugar so that the flavors get mixed, stirring at the same time so that the rice doesn't stick. Stir for five minutes and scrape the inside of the vanilla pod adding it to the mixture. For more flavor you can add 1 teaspoon of grated lime peel and also a cup of shredded coconut.

"My grandmother's house was filled with the intense aroma of vanilla as she made this dessert."

Mexican Quesadillas

NATHALY ROSAS, MEXICO

Quesadillas are an easy dish that anyone can make in their house on a cold night, when there are guests in your home, or it can be a simple snack. I made quesadillas when I visited my cousin because we did not know how to cook, so we made quesadillas. You can make them in two different ways: First you can buy the tortillas and heat them in the microwave. However, the effort to make quesadillas more slowly will result in a much better and flavorful quesadilla. You should take your time.

FOR TEN SERVINGS

Ingredients:

MASA OF TORTILLAS
- 1 cup of corn flour (masa harina)
- ½ cup of warm water
- 1 teaspoon of salt

SALSA
- 4 tomatoes
- ¼ of a large onion
- 3 cloves of garlic
- 4 red peppers

ADD
- ½ pound of cheese, Mexican cojita or traditional quesillo cheese is best
- ½ pound of ham

Directions:

If you want the fast way to make quesadillas you can buy the tortilla and the salsa. Next put cheese and ham over the tortilla, then put it in the microwave.

If you want the slow, but preferable method, first you need to make the tortillas. For this you need to mix the corn flour, warm water and salt, knead the masa in a bowl, then divide this into small balls, about the size of your fist and knead until they are flat and circular shapes.

The next step is how to make the salsa: first put the tomatoes, red peppers, onions and garlic in the blender then fry the salsa in a pan for 5 minutes with a tablespoon of olive oil. Add salt to taste. When the tortillas and salsa are ready, put the tortillas in a flat pan, then add cheese and ham over the tortilla and let the cheese melt. Best eaten with fresh salsa.

Pupusas from El Salvador

WILBERT ALEXANDER ANAYA MURCIA, EL SALVADOR

Pupusas are the traditional food of El Salvador. They are easy to make. You can make them at home. My mom makes them every weekend. I remember when she made these in my country, I remember the aroma of melting cheese that came out from the kitchen, the sound of the dough as it grew, and the smell of the ingredients coming together. This is a lovely dish. When you try them you will fall in love with them. My mom is a Pupusa specialist, making them with love. They taste delicious.

THIS IS FOR 20 PUPUSAS

Ingredients:

THE BEANS
- 3 cups red beans (cooked)
- 1/4 small onion
- 1/2 cup corn oil
- 1 tablespoon salt
- 1 cup water (my mom use cooking liquid from the beans)

THE CHEESE
- 3 lbs mozzarella cheese(shredded); mozzarella is fine but traditional cheese is even better
- 1/2 green bell pepper (diced)
- 1/2 cup lorocco which is a tropical flower found in Latin markets

THE MASA
- 4 cups masa corn flour (I use Maseca brand)
- 2 cups warm water

Directions:

After mixing the masa harina with water to form a dough, cover the bowl with a clean towel and let stand for 10 minutes. Then with lightly oiled hands roll it into balls. Make an indentation with your thumb, and fill with cheese and the other ingredients. Seal the ball, then pat it into a round disk. Fry it up in oil until browned on both sides, and serve warm. Often pupusas are served with curtido (a cabbage side dish with carrots, onion, vinegar and spices).

Hinjo: Burmese Chicken Soup

Kum Hnin, Burma

This is a Burmese dish that serves sick people or those who can't eat plain cooked rice. When I eat this dish, I recall my grandparents. When I got sick they always cooked it for me. I can still smell the bright ginger and when I remember this dish in my country, I feel better. In 2010, I got sick, but no one cooked this soup for me, so I missed my grandparents at that time. My mom bought it from a store, but it didn't taste the same.

Serves enough for 2 to 4 people

Ingredients:

- 4 cups of water
- 2 cups of rice
- 2 inches of chopped fresh ginger, approx. 1/8 of a cup
- 2 teaspoons salt
- Half of a chicken
- 1 cup of broccoli florets

Directions/Method:

1. Pour water into the pot with 2 cups of rice at the same time-
2. Chop chicken into small pieces
3. Put it into a large pot with the rice
4. Chop broccoli and put it into pot too
5. Stir for 2 minutes, adding in the ginger
6. When rice is ready to eat, pour 2 teaspoons of salt into the pot

Zawngtah:* Burmese Tree Beans with Tilapia

KANG PU, BURMA

Tree beans, *Parkia roxburghii*, are a lesser known nutritious, leguminous tree that grows luxuriantly in Northeast India and Southeast Asia. It is found in India, Bangladesh, Burma (Myanmar), Thailand and the Malaysian region. My grandpa always prepared this dish for us in Tuimang in Burma; we enjoyed eating this for dinner. I remember when my grandpa cooked this for us, I remember the strong scent of onions. We mashed the potatoes with the Zawngtah and flavored them with crisp fried onions, red chili and garlic chives. Zawngtah can also be cooked with fish. Tilapia taste great when cooked with Zawngtah or tree beans.

FOR 4 TO 6 SERVINGS

Ingredients:

- 2 tablespoons peanut oil
- 1 onion medium
- 1 cup of ginger and garlic paste—make this with a ½ cup chopped garlic and a ½ cup chopped fresh ginger, combined with 1 tablespoon of olive oil or as needed to make a paste
- 1½ pounds of tree beans
- 2 medium potatoes
- ¾ cup of fresh peas
- ¼ teaspoon each jeera powder* and dhania powder*
- ½ teaspoon of chili powder
- 4 cups of water
- 1½ pounds of Tilapia

*Zawngtah *or tree beans, for information on this fascinating ingredient see below, and for more detail go to:* https://en.wikipedia.org/wiki/Parkia_peciosa

*jeera powder *is ground cumin and* *dhania *powder is ground coriander; they are often ground together into one spice powder. They are frequently used in Southeast Asian and Indian cooking. (Wikipeida)*

Method

1. Scrape the skin off of the beans (a skilled job, which is best outsourced to clean the fresh green skin) with a scraper. Cut into half inch pieces.

2. Fry onions till golden brown in 2tbsp of peanut oil, add ginger garlic paste.

3. Add potatoes cut into slices, add ¾ cup of fresh peas, add the Zawngtah (tree beans).

4. Sauté for 5 minutes and add jeera powder and dhania powder.

5. Add ½ teaspoon of chili powder.

6. Sauté on low heat for 5 minutes and add water.

7. Let water boil for 5 minutes and add the fish.

8. Add salt to taste.

9. Let simmer for ten minutes.

10. Garnish with fresh coriander and serve.

The beans or other Parkia species (Parkia javanica and Parkia singalaris for example) are popular as a culinary ingredient in Indonesia, Malaysia, Singapore, Laos, southern Thailand, Burma, and northeastern India. They are sold in bunches, still in the pod, or the seeds are sold in plastic bags. Pods are gathered from the wild, or from cultivated trees: they are exported in jars or cans, pickled in brine, or frozen. In marketplaces, depending on the country of origin Parkia species may be labelled peté, petai, yongchaa, Zawngtah in Zomi, or Zawngtah (pronounced Zongtrah) among Mizo. They are best when combined with other strongly flavored foods such as garlic, ginger, and chili peppers. When young, the pods are flat because the seeds have not yet developed, and they hang like a bunch of slightly twisted ribbons, pale green, almost translucent. At this stage they may be eaten raw, fried or pickled. Young tender pods with undeveloped beans can be used whole in stir-fried dishes. (Wikipedia)

Mohinga: Burmese Fish Noodle Soup

AUNG AUNG, BURMA

In my family, we eat Mohinga that my mother always prepared when we lived in Yangon city. I remember the strong scent of ginger and onion as they sung together in the frying pan. I can still hear my mother telling us stories of how her mother taught her to make Mohinga when she was a teenager. This Mohinga is usually made with small river catfish known in Burma as nga gyi (sturgeon), nga ku (catfish), or nga khonn ma (barbus fish) which I believe are related to the Pangas catfish.

Ingredients:

- ½ cup peanut oil
- 1 tsp turmeric powder
- ½ red onion, finely sliced
- 1 stalk lemongrass
- 1 one inch piece of ginger, finely chopped
- 3 cloves of garlic finely chopped
- 1/3 cup shrimp paste
- 1 tsp sweet paprika
- 3 Tbsp. cooked, crushed chickpeas
- 1/3 cup toasted rice powder
- 4 Tbsp. fish sauce
- 3 boiled eggs, sliced
- ½ cup boiled banana trunk (alternatively, use banana blossom)
- Pinch of dried chili flakes

Directions/Method:

Put enough fish to serve a nice meal for family of four in a large pan, add the water, lemongrass and turmeric. Bring to a boil and simmer for 6-10 minutes until the fish is just cooked. Remove the fish from the pan and when cool enough to handle, peel the skin and flake the flesh, discarding any bones. Drain the fish stock through a sieve and reserve for the soup.

Pound the onion, garlic, ginger, dried chilies and lemongrass into a paste in a pestle and mortar, otherwise just chop everything as finely as you can.

To serve, put a handful of noodles in a bowl and ladle over the soup. Let everyone add the garnishes as they wish. It should taste spicy, salty and tangy from the limes. (lime, coriander, basil, dried chili peppers for garnish)

Julianna's version of Mohinga: Burmese Fish Noodle Soup

JULIANNA MOE, BURMA

This is a popular dish in Burma. We always eat this when we celebrate a birthday or a festival. But my dad made this for our family and friends. They came to our house and enjoyed this dish. When I eat this dish, it reminds me of Malaysia when my friend had a birthday party. All of her friends and my friends went to her birthday and we played games, and watched horror movies. It was one of the best days of my life.

IT CAN SERVE 5 PEOPLE

Ingredients:

- 1 Tbsp. vegetable or canola oil
- 1 onion, finely diced
- 1 tsp ginger, crushed
- 1 tsp turmeric
- 2 Tbsp. shrimp paste
- 2 red chilies, chopped
- 60g (2oz) banana stem, sliced thinly
- 2 stalks of lemongrass, sliced thinly
- 675ml (3 cups) fish stock
- 50g (2oz) flour
- 50g (2oz) rice, toasted and ground
- 500g (1lb) dried thin rice noodles
- 200g (7oz) firm white fish, such as haddock, pollack or sea bass, sliced

Lime wedges, fried onions, extra chopped chilies and fresh coriander leaves (cilantro) to serve.

Directions

1. Heat oil in saucepan. Add the onion, the garlic, the ginger, the fresh lemongrass (finely chopped or 1 tsp of ground lemon grass), the chili powder, and the turmeric to the oil. Cook on medium heat until fragrant.

2. Add water, shrimp paste, onions, and ground toasted rice. Mix well, bring to a boil, and stir thoroughly to remove lumps. Once thickened, reduce to a simmer for 20 minutes.

3. Cut fish into chunks, add to the soup, mix, and cook for another 10 minutes.

4. On the side, boil water and add rice noodles for 5 minutes, until tender, and drain.

5. Serve soup on the noodles with garnishes.

An ttam thor: Burmese Mustard Greens with Rice

CECILIA DAWT IANG, BURMA

In my family we eat this dish for lunch and dinner. My mom always prepared this dish for us in Hakha Chin. I remember when my mom made this. I can still hear her pounding the onion on the kitchen table. We enjoyed eating this at lunch with hot rice. It is best to cook this dish in the summer when the vegetables are the freshest.

SERVES FOUR

Ingredients:

- Mustard greens—two large bunches
- 2 cups uncooked rice
- 1 Tablespoon peanut oil
- ½ teaspoon salt
- 2 Tablespoons chopped cilantro
- 1 onion medium—cut into pieces
- Chili pepper flakes (to taste)

Directions/Method:

1. First wash the mustard greens and put in the sun to dry. After the mustard greens are dried cut or tear them into ½ inch pieces. The mustard greens usually take two days to dry depending on the intensity of the sun and heat.

2. Next make the rice soup. Measure the rice into a pot and add 6 cups of water. Bring to a boil over high heat. Cover the pot. Lower heat to a simmer and cook until rice is tender, 20 minutes.

3. Take the chopped pieces of mustard greens and put in them in a jar with the rice soup. Add chili pepper, salt, and oil and put it in the jar. This stays in the covered jar in the sun or in a warm place for one week.

4. The dish will now be ready. Eat with cooked rice and garnish with chopped onion, extra peanut oil and fresh cilantro.

Recipe for Somali Tea

MALAAK ABDALLAH, SOMALIA

*"I cannot imagine my life,
even for a day, without Somali tea".*
—from my poem about Somali tea!

SERVES 10 LARGE CUPS OF TEA OR 15 SMALL CUPS

Somali Tea, Ingredients:

- 10 cups of water
- 1 cup of brown sugar
- 10 cardamom pods
- 10 pieces of cloves
- 1 half teaspoon of cinnamon
- 10 teaspoons of red tea leaves

Method

We boil the water and we add the sugar then we add all the spices, we soak them for 15 minutes in the boiling water and then we put in the tea leaves. When the tea has brewed, strain it from the cooking pot, pour into a large tea pot and serve.

Most often Somali tea is taken with milk. This traditional Somali tea is very sweet and wonderfully spicy.

Nepalese Kheer: Special Rice Pudding

JEEWAN POUDEL, NEPAL

Kheer is prepared for festivals, temples, and all special occasions. The word Kheer and the dish came from Northern India. Originally, the word Kheer may derive from the Sanskrit word *Ksheeram* which means "milk." The first people to make Kheer may have been Middle Eastern, but it is so popular that every Hindu person knows how to make it, as well as those who are not Hindu. My family makes Kheer on special Nepali festivals which are Dashain and Tihar. It is really delicious. Kheer is an ancient name; it is about 2,000 years old.

MAKES 4 TO 6 SERVINGS

Ingredients:

- 1 Tablespoon + 2 teaspoons ghee, clarified butter
- 1 ¼ cup cooked rice
- 2 cups of full fat milk
- ½ cup sweetened condensed milk
- 2 Tablespoons sugar or to taste
- ⅛ teaspoon grated nutmeg powder (called jaiphal in Nepal)
- ½ teaspoon of cardamom
- 1 to 2 teaspoons of saffron threads, soaked in a very small amount of boiling water, or more to taste and for color
- ½ Tablespoon chopped cashew nuts
- ½ Tablespoon chopped almonds
- ½ Tablespoon pistachios

Method:

1. Use a non-stick frying pan to make kheer.

2. Wash rice, changing water until the water appears clear.

3. Melt the butter in a frying pan on medium heat.

4. Add the rice and stir-fry for 2 minutes.

5. Add the milk, cook until the rice is tender and the milk is creamy and reduced to about half. Stir often to ensure the milk does not burn in the bottom of the pan.

6. Add the sugar, nutmeg, saffron, cardamom, almonds and pistachios and let simmer for a few more minutes.

7. Turn off the heat.

8. As kheer cools of will become thicker in texture.

9. Kheer can be served chilled or warm.

Paleu: Nepalese Rice Pudding

MAHENDRA BISWA, NEPAL

In my refugee camp, Khudunabari camp, Nepal. I remember when my mom cooked this dish for us. I can still remember her saying while she cooked, "You should learn to cook because someday you will have to leave us and settle down with your wife and kids." We usually enjoyed eating this in the evening with hot, spicy tomato or potato chutney. Many people in our culture cook this popular dish for weddings or other celebrations. It is best to cook this dish with lots of love and fresh ingredients.

SERVES 8 TO 10 PEOPLE AS A SIDE DISH

Ingredients:

- 2½ cups of Basmati Rice
- 1 Tablespoon Oil
- ½ cup ghee-clarified butter (optional, but strongly advised for a more authentic, tastier recipe. If not used, increase oil by 1 ½ Tbsps.)
- 1 large onion, finely chopped
- ¼ cup fresh green peas and ¾ cup fresh French green beans
- 1 large tomato, chopped
- 1 green chili
- ½ cup Paneer (special cheese can be found in Southeast Asian or Indian markets)
- 1 tsp. to 1 Tbsp. fresh ginger, chopped
- 2 whole cloves
- 2 coriander leaves
- 1 cinnamon stick broken in halves
- 1 small piece of bay leaf
- 1/2 tsp. garam masala powder (traditional spice mixture includes usually includes mace, clove, pepper, cinnamon, coriander and cardamom)
- juice of ½ of lemon or more to taste; optional, 1tsp. of grated lemon rind
- 1 tsp. salt or more to taste

Directions/Method:

1. Wash rice and soak it in the water for 15-12 min

2. Heat ghee and oil together in a pressure cooker

3. Add bay leaf, cinnamon, clove, and sauté for 30 second. Add onion and sauté until it turns light brown

4. Add chopped tomato, green peas, green beans and chopped green chili (stir fry them for approx.)

5. Add soaked rice, garam masala powder, salt and pour lemon and mix them in

6. After 2 minutes, add 31/2 cups of water, stirring well

7. Close the lid and cook it over medium flame for 2 whistles (wait until it whistles)

8. When 1st whistle is completed, reduce the flame to low and cook until another whistle. Add the paneer cheese

9. Turn of the flame and now relax and eat this delicious dish, be sure to remove bay leaves, cloves and cinnamon sticks before serving.

"It is best to cook this dish with
lots of love and fresh ingredients."

Conversations
Students Talk to the Cooks at Project Feast

with a recipe from each cook

IN EARLY NOVEMBER, our students took a short bus ride to the Tukwila Community Center, where we were warmly welcomed by Project Feast staff, with coffee and tea awaiting us. The students interviewed eight Project Feast cooks in teams. They asked each cook questions about her journey to the U.S., about her memories and connections to food and cooking, and about the many benefits of participating in Project Feast. These conversations were recorded by three Jack Straw sound engineers. The day culminated with an enlightening recipe workshop presented by cookbook author Kathleen Flinn, and *seriously* delicious food from the Project Feast cooks.

Mexican Mole Verde with Chicken & Red Rice

By Susana Aca Ramirez

Prep time: 40 minutes
Cooking time: 1 hour 30 minutes

You can find dried pasilla peppers in the Mexican section of well-stocked supermarkets. In a pinch, you can use poblano although the dish won't be quite as spicy. Makes about 10 servings.

- 2 ½ pounds boneless chicken breast
- 1 bunch of cilantro
- 2 teaspoons salt

- 1 cube chicken bouillon
- 3 cups basmati rice
- 8 ounce can crushed tomatoes
- 8 ounce can diced tomatoes

- 4 ounces spinach
- 1 pound tomatillo, husks and stems removed
- Few leaves romaine lettuce
- 4 ounces serrano peppers
- 4 ounces of green onion (about 1 bunch)
- 8 ounces radishes
- 8 ounces pasilla pepper
- 2 cloves garlic
- 1 ¼ bottle mole verde

Put the chicken in six cups of water in a pot with a tight-fitting lid. Add half the cilantro and the salt. Bring to a boil, then cover and turn off the heat. Let rest in the hot water for 15 minutes. Drain the water and save it to use in the sauce and to cook the rice.

For the sauce: Add a bit of all the next nine ingredients plus the rest of the cilantro into a food processor. Do not put just one ingredient at a time in the processor but rather mix it all up in batches, saving the mole verde until the end. Put all the ingredients in a large pot, adding water if needed and simmer for 30 minutes.

Scoop out some of the hot mole to the food processor, removing the cap and placing a cloth over the top. Process with ½-cup of the chicken cooking liquid and the bouillon cube. Put this mixture into a separate pan and simmer for 20 minutes.

Meanwhile, cook the rice according to package instructions, using chicken liquid and the liquid from the two cans of tomatoes in place of water. Add the crushed and diced tomatoes to the rice and cook.

Combine the chicken-broth infused mixture into the original pan. Simmer until it coats the back of a spoon. Add the chicken and heat through. Taste both the sauce and the rice and add salt if needed.

Susana Aca – Mexico

SUSANA ACA was born in Mexico. She moved to the U.S. in 1999 because there were not enough opportunities in Mexico for her and her family. She misses her family and she misses the way her grandma cooked eggs and chicken with her mole. She started cooking when she was twelve years old. Project Feast helps Susana represent Mexico and Mexican culture when she cooks food in her traditional way. When she teaches people how to cook, she feels proud of herself and her culture. Project Feast makes her feel comfortable and she feels it has changed life for many women like her. Susana has made many friends in Project Feast, and now they feel like family.

Susana knows that many women enjoy this Project. The major difference for Susana, in cooking her food in Mexico and the U.S., is that she has a hard time finding the same ingredients here. Through Project Feast Susana has learned to eat different types of food. She has tried Ethiopian food and loves it! When we asked Susanna if she believed that food was a passport for anyone's heart, she answered, "Yes, when the food is really good, maybe people remember when they were young, or they remember their country, or family or a special day."

INTERVIEWED BY MAHENDRA BISWA, JENNIFER ESCOBAR AND SOLOMON DAM

Shakar Lama Cookies—Iraqi Cardamom Nut Cookies

By Taghreed Ibrahim

Prep time: 25 minutes
Cooking time: 15 minutes

Also known as cardamom nut cookies, these popular, fragrant treats are traditionally served with hot, thick Iraqi tea.

Makes about 25 cookies.

- 1 cup butter, softened
- 1 ½ cup superfine sugar
- 2 cups all-purpose flour
- ½ teaspoon ground cardamom
- 1/8 teaspoon salt
- Almonds or hazelnuts for garnish (optional)

Preheat oven to 375 F.

Mix the butter and sugar in a small bowl using an electric mixer until light and fluffy, about 2 minutes. Blend in the flour, cardamom and salt, mixing carefully to incorporate. Using a spoon, form the batter into two dozen small balls, placing each onto a cookie sheet. Flatten each into a cookie and garnish with a single nut. Bake for 10 to 15 minutes or until golden. Allow the cookies to cool completely on the baking sheet before removing to a plate.

Taghreed Ibrahim - Iraq

Taghreed Ibrahim was born and raised in Iraq. She moved to the U.S. in 2013. Taghreed left her country because there was a war and she didn't feel her family was safe because her husband worked in media. Before arriving in the U.S., they moved to Dubai and lived there for four years. She came to the U.S. with the assistance of the IRC. (International Rescue committee). The IRC helped them to get to the U.S., though they had to wait for seven years. The hardest part of leaving her country was that she was separated from her family, but when they arrived in the U.S., she finally felt safe. Her mom taught her how to cook when she was twelve years old. She loves to eat and is inspired by her family. She feels comfortable working with Project Feast and has a lot of fun with her friends there, tasting different culture's foods. Taghreed makes special food for her children and enjoys cooking for her family the most. When she cooks, she is reminded of the markets in her home country.

INTERVIEWED BY MADYAN BAKR, JAMES MUNG, CECILIA DAWT IANG, AND RAM ZA THANG

Orange Iraqi Teatime Cake

By Taghreed Mahmood

Prep time: 25 minutes
Cooking time: 30 minutes

I chose this recipe because it is one of the dishes that I use to introduce people to Iraqi teatime customs. Also, this pastry is one of the fancy items that I cook for my youngest son's birthday. My son is a sophomore at Green River College working to transfer to Seattle University. His goal is to become a surgical nurse. The Iraqi ritual of teatime occurs twice per day, first in the morning and then again in the afternoon from between 4 p.m. to 6 p.m. It is traditional to serve a small sweet with tea.

Makes eight to 10 servings.

- 1 cup unsalted butter, softened, plus more for cake pan
- 2 cups sugar
- 4 eggs
- 3 cups all-purpose flour
- 1 Tablespoon baking powder
- 1 teaspoon salt
- 1 cup fresh orange juice
- 1 teaspoon pure vanilla extract
- 1 teaspoon ground cardamom
- ½ cup walnuts, whole or crushed
- ½ cup raisins
- 1 Tablespoon grated orange zest (from two oranges)
- 2 Tablespoon unsweetened coconut

Preheat oven to 350 F.

Brush the cake pan with butter. Using an electric mixer, cream the butter until fluffy. Add sugar and continue to cream well for 6 to 8 minutes. Add the eggs one at a time, beating just enough to include. Add the flour, baking powder, salt and fresh orange juice alternately to the creamed mixture. Add vanilla and cardamom and continue to beat until mixed. Add walnuts, raisins and orange zest and mix them in. Pour the batter into a standard cake pan, topping with the coconut. Bake for 25 to 30 minutes or until the cake is lightly browned and a toothpick comes out clean from the center. Remove from the oven and cool on a rack. Enjoy your orange cake with tea!

Taghreed Mahmood - Iraq

TAGHREED MAHMOOD was born in Iraq. She came to the U.S. as a refugee in 2013 with the help of the World Relief Organization. She is originally from Baghdad. Due to the war in Iraq her family moved to Turkey and began the process with UNHCR of coming to America. The war caused a painful separation for Taghreed and her family with her with her oldest daughter remaining in Turkey and her oldest son in Libya. She feels that her strength during times of great challenge came from her love for her children. Although she is an accountant many of her successes have come from her love for cooking. She believes that food reflects our culture and that she has found her right path with Project Feast. Through catering and teaching Iraqi cooking classes she has met people from different countries and shared her culture with them. She won a first prize in a cooking competition in Turkey and she has appeared on the Al Jazeera America cable channel to show how she cooks traditional Iraqi dishes. Taghreed says that her dream would come true if she could be back with her family in her country in a time of peace—this would make her the happiest mom in the world.

INTERVIEWED BY AUNG AUNG, ABDIRAHMAN ABDI, MALAAK ABDALLAH, AND JULIANNA MOE

Dormoda—Gambian Peanut Butter Stew

By Naffie Sinyan

Prep time: 20 minutes
Cooking time: 2 hours 30 minutes

The Gambia is a small country in West Africa bounded by Senegal and bordering the Atlantic coast to its left. This dish can also be made without meat by substituting vegetables such as peas and more carrots, yams or acorn squash in place of the chicken. This is often served with white rice, or ceeb in Wolof, which is the name of one of Gabia's largest ethnic groups. Wolof is also the name of the language spoken by Wolof people, whose kingdom once stretched throughout West Africa, and who today live in countries such as Gambia, Senegal, Mauritania and Guinea.

Serves six to eight.

- 1 16 oz. jar of unsweetened, natural peanut butter
- 1 11.5 oz. can of crushed tomatoes
- 4 Tablespoons tomato paste
- 2 small onions, minced
- 1 Tablespoon minced garlic
- ½ teaspoon red chili powder
- 2 chicken bouillon cubes
- 10 chicken legs, lightly salted
- 4 large carrots, cut into 2-inch chunks
- 2 Tablespoons fresh lemon juice
- ¼ salt, more if needed

In a large saucepan or stockpot, bring 8 cups of water to a rolling boil. Add the peanut butter, crushed tomatoes, tomato paste, onions, garlic, chili powder and bouillon cubes and bring it back to the boil. Turn heat down to medium and let simmer for an hour stirring occasionally with a wooden spoon.

Add the chicken, let it simmer for an hour. Add carrots, lemon juice and salt. Cook for about 25 minutes until the carrots are softened. Taste, adding more salt if needed.

Naffie Sinyan - The Gambia

NAFFIE SINYAN was born in The Gambia, a small West African country. She came to the U.S. nearly twenty five years ago when she got married. She has only lived in two countries, The Gambia and the U.S. She learned how to cook from her mother and started to cook when she was fifteen years old. She loves to cook both African and American food for anyone. Project Feast has introduced her to many new people and skills.

Cooking in The Gambia and the U.S. are very different because many of the ingredients she used in The Gambia she cannot find in the U.S. She misses her friends and family who are back in her country very much. She is here with her three daughters, all of whom she is teaching to cook.

INTERVIEWED BY NAINA RAI, ARUN BISWAKARMA, AVNOOR BRAR, & SAGAR RAI

Shrimp Ceviche

By Yngrid Solis

Prep time: 15 minutes
Cook time: 10 minutes

This spicy dish from the Yucatan in Mexico utilizes Tapatio is a hot sauce manufactured in California, but you can substitute your favorite brand if you can't locate it. To "chiffonade" the herbs, roll together and slice thinly.

Makes 12 appetizer servings.

- 2 pounds shrimp
- 1 white onion, diced
- 6 to 8 tomatoes, seeded and diced
- 1 bunch cilantro, chiffonade
- 2 avocados, peeled and diced
- 1 cucumber, peeled and diced
- 2 or 3 ½-inch limes
- 1/3 cup ketchup
- 2 or 3 Tablespoons Tapatio hot sauce, according to taste
- Red pepper flakes
- 2 to 3 teaspoons salt

Boil water in a sauce pot. Add the shrimp and cook just until they turn pink. Drain with a colander. Cut each into 3 pieces. Set aside.

In a large bowl, mix the shrimp and the onions, tomatoes, cilantro, avocados and cucumber, squeeze in the limes, then add the ketchup, hot sauce, 1 to 3 pinches of red pepper flakes and salt. Taste, adjusting seasonings as needed. Serve with corn tortilla chips or crackers.

Yngrid Solis – Mexico

YNGRID SOLIS was born in Yucatan, Mexico. She came to America in 1991 because she wanted to find a better life. She moved to Nebraska to live with her brother and his family, but she felt sad because she left her sister and father in Mexico. She struggles with learning the English language, but enjoys her time in Project Feast. She likes to cook the ceviche her mother taught her to make. She misses her traditional dishes and fresh products. Yngrid told us, "Food is important!"

Project Feast is also important to her because she likes to teach other people about her cultural dishes and meet new friends. Her advice for students is to stay in school to have better opportunities in life.

INTERVIEWED BY HAI NGUYEN, NATHALY ROSAS, WILBERT ANAYA & CINDY DUARTE-REYNOSA

Piroshki

By Inna Stetsenko

Prep time: 3 hours
Cook Time: 20 minutes

This recipe comes from Ukraine. It reminds me of my mother, a professional cook. She always made delicious dishes for us. I use different kinds of filling such as meats, cabbage, berries, poppy seeds, potatoes and even fish. Piroshki can be used as a main dish, for breakfasts or as a snack, just change the size.

MAKES ABOUT THREE DOZEN SMALL HAND-SIZED PASTRIES.

PASTRY

- 2 Tablespoons yeast
- 2 teaspoons sugar
- ¼ cup warm water
- 1 ½ cups warm milk
- 6 Tablespoons butter, melted
- 1 teaspoon salt
- 2 1/2 cups flour

FILLING

- 4 pounds apples, chopped
- ½ cup sugar
- 1 teaspoons cinnamon
- 1 teaspoon vanilla extract
- 1 teaspoon corn starch

Combine the yeast, sugar and warm water to a large bowl of a stand mixer. Let rest for at least five minutes until the yeast blooms. Add the warm milk, melted butter and salt and mix on a low speed. Add the flour and mix until the dough comes together. Cover with plastic wrap and allow to rest for at least an hour or until doubled in size. While the dough rises, make the filling. Toss the apples with the sugar, cinnamon, vanilla and corn starch and set aside.

On a floured surface, roll the dough into fat "snakes" and cut into 2-inch pieces. Roll or press each piece with your hand or a rolling pin so that it's round and flat. Fill with the apple mixture in the center, fold the dough over itself and pinch the edges closed.

Place the stuffed pastries onto a cookie sheet. Brush top of pastry with egg yolk. Allow to rest for 20 to 30 minutes. While they rest, preheat the oven to 350 degrees Fahrenheit. Bake for 20 minutes or until golden brown.

Inna Stetsenko - Ukraine

INNA STETSENKO was born in Ukraine and has been in the United States since 2012. She left Ukraine because it was a dangerous place and her life was difficult there. In the U.S., she struggles with English, but really enjoys cooking. Her mom, who was a professional cook, taught her to cook dishes from all over the world. Whenever Inna cooks, she remembers her mother.

Her passion is to cook her culture's food and to see people happy because of her cooking. She feels Project Feast helps people who are similar to her to improve their English and their cooking skills.

INTERVIEWED BY SMILE KHAI, HELEN BOIH, NINI KHAING & SUSMA RAI

Alicia Doro Wot—Ethiopian Chicken Sauce

By Nebiat Yifru

Wat is a traditional stew or curry from Ethiopia, typically served with the well-known Injera bread, a large flat bread which is often used as an edible "plate" as well. This recipe is different than the more common Key Doro Wot, which contains berbere spice, giving it more of a kick.

Serves about six.

- 2 pounds onion (about 3 large), peeled and diced
- 6 chicken legs
- 1 teaspoon salt
- 2 limes, chopped
- 1/2 cup oil, such as peanut oil
- ½ teaspoon turmeric
- 2 cloves garlic, chopped
- 1 piece of fresh ginger, peeled and chopped
- 6 boiled eggs
- 2 to 3 cups of water or chicken stock
- 1/2 Tablespoon Ethiopian butter (butter with cardamom)

Remove the skin from the chicken legs. Generously sprinkle the meat with salt and rub with the limes. Let sit for about 10 to 15 minutes.

Over medium heat, add the oil to a Dutch oven or a stock pot with a lid. Add the onions, turmeric, garlic and ginger. Cook for about 10 minutes until the onions soften. Reduce the heat to simmer and cook for another half hour until caramelized and golden, adding water as needed to keep the onion mixture from sticking. This is a good time to boil and peel the eggs.

When the onions are caramelized, add the chicken legs to the pan turning to coat in the onion mixture. Add the stock or water, cover and let simmer for about 25 to 30 minutes or until the chicken is tender. Remove the lid and let cook to reduce to a thick consistency, stirring in the butter.

Serve the chicken with wedges of the boiled egg and bread or rice.

Nebiat Yifru - Ethiopia

NEBIAT YIFRU was born and raised in Ethiopia. She came to the United States in 2013 hoping for a better life for her children than she had in Ethiopia. Her grandmother taught her to cook when was she was only five years old. Nebiat loves to make Injera, an Ethiopian bread, and Doro Wet, a very special dish in her culture. Nebiat believes that Project Feast provides a good opportunity to meet new people and learn different kinds of dishes. She also has the opportunity to experience other cultures by sharing her cooking experiences with the other Project Feast participants from all over the world. When she teaches someone else to cook, she feels happy. Cooking and food remind Nebiat of her family and culture. We were able to ask Nebiat some of our questions in Amharic since two of us are also from Ethiopia.

When we asked her about using recipes Nebiat said, "I believe that the cooking knowledge that we get from home is good. But the problem is, we don't use the recipe. We just show somebody how to cook. We don't write it on paper and we don't measure things. I can put one spoon of salt, or two spoons of salt, but if I don't write the recipe, I cannot transfer it to my kids. The good thing of the modern way, or the American way, is that you can transfer anything. Now that I have learned how to write a recipe, I can write any of the knowledge that I got from my mom or from my family so that I can transfer it to other parts of society or the next generation."

INTERVIEWED BY RODAS NEGUSSIE, ABDULREHEIM SHUBA AND KANG PU

Home-style Chinese Pork Ribs

Yanzhi Zhang

Prep time: 15 minutes
Cook time: 20 minutes

Makes three to four appetizer servings.

- 1 ¾ pounds pork spare ribs cut into small pieces
- 2 Tablespoons Chinese cooking wine (any type of rice wine such as Shaoxing cooking wine)
- 1 Tablespoon cornstarch
- 2 teaspoons Chinese vinegar
- 2 Tablespoons vegetable oil
- 1 piece ginger, peeled and minced
- 2/3 cup chopped yellow onion
- 1 clove garlic, crushed
- 6 to 8 Szechwan peppercorns
- 2 pieces of star anise
- 2 Tablespoons water
- 3 Tablespoons light soy sauce
- 2 Tablespoons crystal rock candy
- ¾ cup water
- 1/3 pound baby carrots
- ½ cup chopped yellow or green peppers
- 1 teaspoon Chinese aromatic vinegar (optional)

Combine the ribs with the cooking wine and a cornstarch and let marinade for about 10 minutes. Add the vinegar and let sit for another minute. Add the oil to a large pan over medium-high heat. Add the ginger and then stir in the onion. Stir together for a minute or until the onion is translucent. Add the pork ribs and continue stirring for two minutes until the ribs turn lightly brown on both sides. Add the garlic, peppercorns, star anise, soy sauce, rock candy and water. Stir for several minutes over medium heat uncovered until the sauce reduces by two thirds. Add the carrots and peppers. Cover and cook until the meat is tender and the sauce starts to thicken. You can add the aromatic vinegar at this point for more smell and taste.

Yanzhi Zhang - China

YANZHI ZHANG is from China. She was first introduced to cooking by her mother, who always made special food for her. Yanzhi struggles to live in the U.S. partly because she doesn't speak much English, but she is overcoming her struggles and making friends in Project Feast. Project Feast helps her progress with English and helps her build her cooking skills.

Yanzhi feels that Project Feast helps people to have a better life by helping them share their cultures with others through food. Yanzhi really misses the spicy chicken of her country and loves sweet and sour flavors the most.

INTERVIEWED BY KUM HINN, EBENEZER LIAN, SAMA JABBARIMEHMANI, & ZAKARIA KAHIN

A Basket of Fruits and Vegetables

Avocado

People love it
people hate it
it tastes like the creamy clouds
of the sky
it smells like
the wet earth.
Green inside
black outside,
impeccable heart
giving life.
Fruit or vegetable,
no one knows.
Each bite is gorgeous
exquisite flavor.
People hate it
people love it,
but no one really knows
what it is.

NATHALY ROSAS, MEXICO

Avocado

Avocado
black and green
sweet and creamy
best if shared
mixed with sugar and ice
or eaten in a sandwich
folks of different languages
love and like it
cut it in half
get stuck in the middle
moving as a circle
then it breaks in half
take the sharp knife
a strong stab in the seed
take it out and hold the spoon
and empty it.

VU NGUYEN, VIETNAM

Carrots

The orange carrot of tropical night
Look carefully, the morning wakes the carrots up!
What a lovely vegetable, so much like the orange moon.

CINDY DUARTE-REYNOSA, GUATEMALA

The Chili

The chili tastes like burning cotton,
that you can't take back,
it changes like the seasons,
It feels like a huge, soft blanket
that you wear on a cold night.
The chili belongs on your table,
you think you don't need any more summer
or heat, but that's chili,
motivating your belief
for your next step.

KANG PU, BURMA

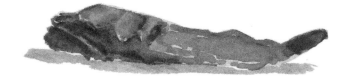

169

Cauliflower

It has a deeply white color
a color that makes me feel sympathetic
to another.
When I see it, I remember my mother,
my mother's honest heart is as white as cauliflower.
The white cauliflower tastes of beautiful dreams

AUNG AUNG, BURMA

Cucumber

When I see the small cucumber
it reminds me if what my mom told me
the day I was born, that the sky cried.
The small cucumber has tears
 on the outside and small thorns,
Yes, the cucumber looks tough and mean
on the outside,
but inside it tastes like drinking water
in the sunshine,
like that, do not judge people badly,
by how they look on the outside.

CECILIA DAWT IANG, BURMA

Cucumber

The cucumber tastes like sweet water,
and like a person walking in the Himalayas,
that the person could keep walking,
it softly lights up our faces,
and the very air smells fresh.

NAINA RAI, NEPAL

Mangoes

The mango tastes sweet like a good couple
in the same heart.
Look at it carefully,
it is the sun shining in the evening!

ARUN BISWAKARMA, NEPAL

The mango tastes like stars in the sky,
Look at it, it is like the earth's green land,
What a tasty fruit,
It has love in its heart!

SAGAR RAI, NEPAL

Yes, the mango tastes like the sweet
of my grandmother's fresh garden.
That's it! The color is like springtime grass.

RAM ZA THANG, BURMA

The mango tastes like
the sweetness of my vacation
on the beach.
That's a sweet mango!
What a delicious fruit, so much like
the sun going down.

HAI NGUYEN, VIETNAM

Oranges

The orange tastes like the sweetness of loving,
With its smell like walking in the morning to church
And the big sky in the evening sunshine.
Those times I remember you,
Every single day, not matter what,
You are inside my heart.

RODAS NEGUSSIE, ETHIOPIA

Fruits of Love

The strawberry tastes like your lips
when I feel your lips with my lips
it makes millions of strawberries
on my lips.

The watermelon is like your kisses,
sweet and juicy.

And the mango is like our love
because our sweet love spreads
to everyone's mouth.

ROBERTO DIAZ, MEXICO

You taste like stars in the dark sky
You smell like the morning light
You are the color of the evening sky,
You feel like the velvet of a bird's feathers,
You fill the morning air with your song.

MADYAN BAKR, IRAQ

Orange, you sound like listening to classical violin in the forest,
Every night I dream about you,
One day I will play my violin for you,
One orange autumn day when the world is fresh.

SAMA JABBARIMEHMANI, IRAN

Eggplant

My eggplant tastes like having a romance
in a beautiful land,
It is the color of a fall morning,
It feels like a smooth rock,
It smells of fresh air,
It sounds like rock music,
It is so much like sunshine in the morning.

MAHENDRA BISWA, NEPAL

Pineapple

The pineapple, tastes like a sweet voice saying good morning.
It is the color of wintertime with the sun shining in the morning,
it feels like an old man's whiskers, rough, that hurt;
it sounds like peace, motivating and inspiring.

KANG PU, BURMA

Apple

I am an apple
I grow in a garden of two colors
Green, like a leaf,
I hide in the leaves like the night moon.
I smell like the evening sun
And I sound like a silent morning.
I enjoy my life in the garden,
But sometimes I fall from my tree
Hungry to take water from my brother.

AVNOOR BRAR, INDIA

175

Rambutan

You are so annoying and
hairy like a girl
who never washes her hair.

Look at you carefully
and I see you like my angel,

It's hard to say to you, "I love you,"

When I break you
you are sunshine,
soft and sweet to me,
it's hard to leave you alone,
everybody wants to steal you
millions in the world want you,
but they can't have you,
because you belong to me.

KUM HNIN, BURMA

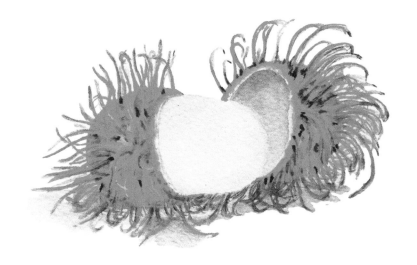

Rambutans are a close relative to the lychee nut. Although they are larger, they offer a similar firm, grapelike texture. Rambutan's most exciting characteristic is their furry outer skin, which makes them look like fresh lychees' punk-rock brother. The Rambutan is native to the Malay-Indonesian region and other regions of tropical Southeast Asia. (Wikipedia)

Watermelon

The Watermelon tastes as sweet as the girl I love,
it is the color of red when her face is in anger,
and green as the grass field we sit in
when we are together.
When I eat the watermelon, I feel like swimming
with my love in the hot summer.

Vu Nguyen, Vietnam

White Dragon Fruit

Dragon fruit of passion
With its delicious flesh of sweetness
White, with tiny black seeds of explosion,
Delightful flavor, so soft and sensual.

Hy Cao, Vietnam

177

About the Poets

Biographies and Portraits

ABDIRAHMAN MOHAMED ABDI was born in Somalia. He came to America when he was eleven years old. In his Muslim religion, there is one God with many names. Abdirahman is one of the names that mean "God" in the Somali language. Abdi speaks two languages, Somali and English. He arrived in America on December 12, 2011. He always wanted to be a basketball, football or soccer player. Abdi also wants peace in his home country.

One food that he misses is *sambusa*. He believes that food rations are never enough. He also believes that taking care of camels, cows and goats is a lot like taking care of other people.

ABDULREHIM ALI SHUBA was born in Oromia, Ethiopia. He is fifteen years old. His first name means "slave of god" in the Arabic language that is spoken by people all over the world. Abdulrehim moved to America on May 15, 2015. He can speak Oromo and Amharic and he is learning English and Arabic.

His dream is to be proud of himself by doing good things and his dream is to be loved by God. Abdulrehim misses many sweet things about his cultural foods such as *doro wet, caccabsaa, dhanga, marqa, kitfo, shakakaa, injera,* and *malawa.* He is proud because of his good manners and his respect for everyone.

Abdulrehim believes that food is good for everyone. He believes that the cultural value of food can help solve his nation's problems. He also believes that rice remembers his mouth every Ramadhan and he believes that *doro wet* is the best food from the culture of his Ethiopian people.

ARUN BISWAKARMA was born in Nepal. He is eighteen years old. For fifteen years, Arun lived in Khudunabari refugee camp. After that, he lived in Pathari refugee camp with 12,000 people. He speaks three languages: Nepali, English and a little bit of Hindi. His life in the refugee camp was very difficult, in part because he could not get a quality education, though his family knew how much education would be important in his life.

He has many dreams, but his family did not have enough money to support his dreams for a good education. He came to the U.S. to make a bright future for himself. He arrived in the USA on November 12, 2014. He is proud of being Nepalese. He has dreams of helping both poor and homeless people who live in Nepal. He believes that everyone should eat *MoMo*. And he believes that food can give joy to everyone.

AVNOOR SINGH BRAR was born in 36 F village in Rajasthan India. He came to America less than six months ago. He lived for fourteen years in India. He speaks three languages: Hindi, English, and Punjabi. He is thankful and proud to be a Sikh. He came to the U.S. to become a singer and a writer, but his main goal is to become a software engineer.

He remembers many foods from his country like *gulgule* vegetables. He wants to eat food that his grandmother and mother made for him. He believes that food makes life happy. He also believes that food brings the taste and smell of your country or city back to you in your memories—that food takes a person back to their memories of home. And he believes that nobody in this world should be hungry.

Cindy Daniela Duarte-Reynosa was born in Guatemala on October 9, 1996. She lived in Guatemala Escuintla, Nueva Concepción for fourteen years. Her mother celebrated her fifteenth birthday with a big party. Her mother decided to go to the USA for a better life with her brother. Cindy came to the USA on June 19, 2013. When she came to the USA life was difficult for her because she didn't understand English very well. Now she understands English better and enjoys living in the USA. She believes that marimba music and the traditional food of her people are what make Guatemala unique.

Dal Lam Kang (Kang Pu) was born in a small village called Tuimang, part of the Zogam region. He is sixteen years old and he has three brothers and one sister. They are still in Burma. He grew up knowing all about farming because that was his dad's work. Kang Pu speaks five languages including Zomi, Mizo, Burma, Malaysian and English.

He lived in Tuimang for thirteen years and then moved to Malaysia in 2011. Kang Pu could not get a good quality education in his country, because his family didn't have enough money to pay for school. When he was ten years old his mom passed away. After that, he wanted to start to find money; that's why he went to Malaysia. In Malaysia, Kang Pu got a job at Pat Kin Pat Sun Cafe Chinese Restaurant. During that time he was only thirteen years old. It was truly hard for him to depart from his family, because he is the only one who went to Malaysia by himself. Kang Pu came to the United States in 2014, with his uncle.

His memories of foods from Burma are corn, vegetables and potatoes. Foods that he always remembers remind him of his country and his mom. Kang Pu often thinks of his mom when he feels hungry, but he knows he cannot let those memories make him too sad. In the future he wants to become a businessman to help his family, and to help his country to become a peaceful country. Kang Pu is thankful for the government in the U.S., because he can get a free education. He really wants to achieve his goals. He believes that his father's *vege* porridge was amazing; it brought all of his family together at meal times.

Kang Pu can't forget his country's food and traditions because his cultural foods are already in his blood. Also, food can save people and food reminds him to honor and keep his culture. Kang Pu believes everyone can do one thing in their life that they dream of, because everybody matters and everybody has different skills.

Dawt (Cecilia) Iang, age fifteen, was born in Hakha, Chin State in Burma. She lived in Hakha for eleven years and then moved to Malaysia in 2012. She came to Seattle in 2014. She speaks three languages. She is Christian and proud to be Christian. Cecilia's dreams are to become an air hostess and singer. She also hopes to make her parents proud of her and no matter how hard her life is, she will always try to be happy.

She misses her country and her country's food. Someday she hopes that she can go back to her country. She misses the food that was grown in her grandmother's garden and the food that her grandmother cooked for her. Whenever she prays, she always prays for her grandmother to stay healthy. Cecilia believes that the taste of good food can change lives. She also believes that sharing food can build friendships.

*Editorial apology: This should read **Cecilia Dawt Iang.**

Ebenezar Lian was born in Burma. He moved to Mizo when he was one year old, and stayed there until he was six. He moved again to India and stayed for nearly three years. He speaks Chin, Mizo, Falam and English. When he was eleven he moved to the U.S. He always hoped to come to the U.S. and he dreams of being a football player.

What he misses the most are his grandparents, his country and the mango tree from his grandma's garden. Ebenezar believes that no people should live with hunger. He believes that people will have enough food if they share their food. He also believes that food brings people together and that food brings enjoyment.

Hai Nguyen was born in Ho Chi Minh City. He lived in Vietnam for fourteen years and then moved to Seattle with his parents. When he came from Vietnam, he could not speak English very well. But now, he can speak English because he has been living in the U.S. for six months. He has now traveled around Seattle and other places so he can speak English very well.

This year, his dreams and goals are following him and he needs to achieve his goals by himself. His goals are to go to college. He hopes to become an engineer in the future to help his country and his family. He will not let himself down and he is a good person. Hai believes that he can achieve his goals and that when something bad happens to him he can overcome it. He believes that everyone should have enough food. Hai also believes that the Vietnamese foods his mom cooks are delicious. Hai believes that food is a weapon that gives people power.

Helen Kim Boih was born in Bukphil which is part of Myanmar. She is seventeen years old. She speaks Mizo, Zomi, and English. In 2011, on July 27, Helen arrived in America. In Zomi, Helen means "candle light," Kim means "you are always there," and Boih means "like a baby."

Helen's goal is to become a dentist because in her country there are many people who don't have healthy teeth. When she grows up she wants to go back and help her country. Helen dreams of helping others, and she always wants to show a smile on her face.

One thing she can never forget is her grandmother's garden and how it grew. Helen is thankful and proud of her brother who graduated in 2015. He is first in her family to graduate. Helen believes that gardens keep our stomachs and our lives full and that if you have a garden you will have enough food for your family. She believes gardens are like a child you have to care for in order to raise amazing food.

Hy Gia Dai Cao was born in Ho Chi Minh City. He speaks Vietnamese and English. He came to America one year ago. He wants to graduate high school and study in college. He ate beef, rice, pork and pho in his country. He misses his friends, his house, his food and his church. He believes that the rice and pho in Vietnam are the best in the world.

JAMES MUNG was born in small village in Burma called Zogam. He lived in Burma for ten and a half years and then moved to the U.S. with his whole family. When he came to America it was a winter day with many cold winds blowing against his body. He will never forget that day in 2011.

James loves school and wants to become a proficient soccer player. He hopes to help poor people someday. James's dream is to go back to Zogam. He believes that he will become a soccer player.

JEEWAN POUDEL was born in Nepal. He is sixteen years old. His name means "life." He was raised in a refugee camp and he is Hindu. He speaks Nepali and English. He came to America in 2009, but he had dreams for a long time to come to America. Now that he is in America, he wants to accomplish his goal to become a computer hardware engineer. Also, one day he wants to go back to Nepal. He is proud to be Nepalese.

Jeewan believes that everyone should have a family. He also believes that when you drink milk you can grow tall. Jeewan believes that everyone should have an education and he believes that there is God in the world. Jeewan says that when you run it helps your body calm you down with your problems. He also believes that everyone should have a home to live in and he believes that when we get mad with one another, food can bring us back together again.

JENNIFER ESTELA ESCOBAR MEJIA was born in San Salvador, El Salvador. She lived in San Jose Los Delgados for eleven years. She speaks two languages: Spanish and English. She moved to the U.S. on May 11, 2011. Her dream is to become a nurse, and she hopes that she can help many people. Her family's dream for her is that she can become a teacher. She likes to cook and she cooks pupusas and tamales, which are the typical food for her country El Salvador.

She misses her country's food, *pasteles, orchata, tamales, panes rellenos,* and *pupusas.* Her grandmother loves to cook for her and her older sisters. The food that her grandma likes to cook grows in her garden. Her grandparents like to grow *maiz, frijoles,* bananas trees and *oloroco.* She believes that the food that she cooks from her country gives her family togetherness and celebration.

Jennifer feels thankful and proud of her dad because her dad makes her laugh when she is sad. Her dad and grandparents inspire and encourage her to keep working hard. She believes that food has the power to bring groups of people and families together. She also believes food has the power that can inspire many teenagers to cook. And Jennifer believes that there should be enough food for children and families everywhere. She believes that no one should suffer from hunger and that food makes people remember their countries and culture.

JULIANNA MOE, age fourteen, was born in Burma. She speaks Chin and Burmese languages. She lived in Burma for seven years and then moved to Malaysia so that her parents could find better jobs. After living in Malaysia for three years, they decided to move to the United States for better education and a better future. After arriving in the United States, it was hard for her to adjust a new place, a new school, and a new language.

Julianna always hopes that one day she can speak English like kids who were born here. She also hopes that she will have someone who stays by her side and who understands her. She has a dream that one day she will be a fashion designer and she will help poor people by giving them clothes and money. After living in the United States for a few years, she thinks about her country where she grew up and she misses her grandma who used to cook chicken soup for her. She hopes that she can visit Burma in the future. Julianna believes that food brings her memories back from her childhood.

KUM THAWNG HNIN was born in a small village in the Chin region of Burma. His name means "two thousand" (2000). His grandpa gave him this name because in his village he was the first to be born on 01/01/2000. Kum went to Malaysia when he was ten years old. He lived in Malaysia for four years before he came to the USA. Life in Malaysia was scary because there were a lot of gangs and rapes. The tongues he speaks are Chin, Burmese and English.

Kum is hoping that he can become one of the successful sons in his family and his village. Kum misses the corn that his grandparents cooked and grew for him. Kum likes to watch corn turn white to yellow when his grandparents put the corn into hot water. He believes people can't live without food. He also believes that his aunt's chicken can bring peace to his family. Kum believes food banks can help give people peace. He also believes that if everyone had enough food, it would help bring peace. Kum believes food is an important reminder of his cultural traditions.

MADYAN BAKR was born in Iraq. He came to America on June 20, 2014. He speaks Kurdish and Arabic and he is learning English. When he left Iraq he went to Jordan, then to Egypt, and then he came to America. His dream was to live in America and his goal was to study in America. He is proud to be Yazidi and from Kurdistan, Iraq.

Mdyan believes that everyone in the world should have enough food. He believes that his culture's *Tashreb* is the best and he believes that food can bring people together.

MAHENDRA BISWA was born in Khudunabari refugee camp in Nepal. He came to America when he was just twelve years old. When he came to America it was a summer day with sunshine in the sky. He is fifteen years old now. For twelve years, he lived in a refugee camp with 15,000 other people. In his free time he spent days with his friends going into the forest and bringing birds from their nests, usually to sell the birds to other people. Mahendra can speak three languages: Nepali, Hindi, and English.

He always dreams and hopes to become a good doctor, so that he can help other poor people. The place where he lived in Nepal didn't have a good education because they lived in a refugee camp and the camp didn't have a good education. His life in the refugee camp was difficult because they didn't have much money to wear good clothes and eat good food.

He mostly misses food from his country that his mom cooked called *bhat* (rice-and-water dough, vegetable, lentil chutney). And he also misses food called *pulao* (pilaf). Mahendra is proud of being in the U.S. because here he doesn't have a difficult time. In Nepal he had a difficult time living in the refugee camp.

MALAAK ABDALLAH was born in Somalia and raised in Saudi Arabia. Her first name means "Angel." She speaks three languages: Somali, Arabic and English. Malaak's mother is from Somalia and her father is from Yemen. Malaak's goal is to work very hard because her dream is to become a dermatologist and have enough money to help the refugees in her home country.

She believes that countries are responsible for their people and should provide food for the people. She also believes that food takes people back to their culture, background and country. And she believes food is the only way to show her culture and who she is to others.

NAINA RAI was born in Beldangi-2 Jhapa Nepal, in a refugee camp. She is sixteen years old. She lived in Nepal for fourteen years as a refugee and then moved to the USA with her whole family through IOM, which helps refugee people. She spent those years in a bamboo and plastic hut. Her life in the refugee camp was very difficult because she could not get a quality education. Naina has many dreams including becoming a teacher or an air hostess. She wants to be a trustworthy daughter for her parents and trusted by all friends and all people who know her. Naina arrived in America on July 9, 2014. She speaks two languages: Nepali and English.

The food she misses from her country is called *dhal/mam* with chicken curry with many spices. Her mom cooked it for her. Naina's goals are to graduate from high school and go to college for four years, then she hopes to find a good job and support her family. She hopes to become a good dancer in the future. Naina is proud to be Nepalese. She also dreams of helping orphan children and poor families. Naina believes that fruits gives us energy. She also believes that the Nepali flag has power to bring back memories. She believes that there should be equal rights for everyone.

NATHALY ROSAS MARTINEZ was born in Minnesota, in the U.S., though she grew up in Mexico where she lived in Veracruz for thirteen years. In 2014, at age fifteen, she moved back to the U.S. only with her mother. She speaks two languages: English and Spanish. In her country she saw all kinds of food because her family likes to cook things like tacos, salsas, *sopes, chileatoles, y picaditas,* and they also like to cook new things. She hopes to go back to her Mexico in 2016.

She is proud of her culture because she thinks that in her culture there are many special traditions. She would like to share her experience of being Mexican with the world. Two of the most important goals in her life are to go to college in Veracruz where she grew up and to support her little brother to achieve his dreams. Nathaly believes that food is our identity and our force, and that our cultural food is our principal source. She believes that each bite of our food has memories of our nation and that food is an important piece of our traditions. Nathaly also believes that food is the blood and soul of our ancestors and that every culture should be proud of its food. And she believes that making food is an art and a way of expressing our memories.

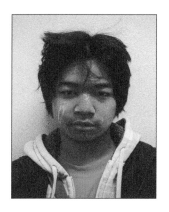

NGA REH was born in Thailand in 2000. He is fifteen years old. For nine years he lived as a refugee. In 2009, he moved to the U.S. so that he could fulfill his dream to have a better life. He first moved to Iowa, but now resides in Seattle. Nga Reh is a new student at Foster High School. His recent arrival here was in November of 2015. He feels that his heart moves like the wind.

NINI KHAING was born in Thailand. She is fifteen years old. Her name means "a warm environment." She speaks three languages: Burmese, Thai, and English. For twelve years, Nini lived in Thailand. She came to America when she was only thirteen years old. She moved to the U.S. in 2012. Her first goal is to do well in art. Her second goal is to help her mom cook, and her third goal is to have A's in all of her classes. To have A's she has to be a responsible person. Her parents really encourage her to go to college and have a good career.

Her favorite food is *Kanom jeen*. *Kanom jeen* is a Thai dish, but it is originally from ancient Burma. In America, it is difficult to find the ingredients for *Kanom jeen*. One day she asked her grandmother to give her a special recipe for Burmese *Kanom jeen*, because her grandmother was born in Myanmar and her grandmother was really good at cooking. Nini believes that she should eat food from the earth, not from the store, because it fresh and clean. She believes that when she eats chicken fried rice, it gives her more ideas for her school work. She also believes that food from the garden is bright, fresh, and clean, but food from the grocery store, though clean, is not as healthy as from a garden. Nini feels that that every culture's food is important.

RAM ZA THANG, age fourteen, was born in Burma. He lived in a small village for eight years and then moved to Malaysia in 2008. He speaks Chin and English. He came to America in 2012. He hopes to become a football player. He likes to listen to Elvis Presley because he likes rock 'n' roll. He misses his house, made out of wood; the color was brown and the roof was made from steel. Also, he misses all of his friends from his country. He believes that food can make people happy. Ram Za also believes that no one should suffer from hunger.

ROBERTO CARLOS AGUILERA DIAZ was born in Aguascalientes, Mexico. He came to America when he was twelve years old. His first name means "shining fame." Roberto speaks three languages: English, Spanish, and Portuguese. He came to the USA on September 3, 2012. Roberto dreams of becoming a pilot.

The foods he misses are the tamales, tortas, pozole and menudo his grandma cooked for him. Roberto's grandfather grew fruits and vegetables in his garden in Aguascalientes.

Roberto has many beliefs about food, such as children should never be hungry. He believes that people go crazy when they don't have enough to eat. He also believes that food brings many families together and he believes that food can solve problems within a family. When poor people are hungry, Roberto believes it brings loneliness, because they don't have enough food.

RODAS NEGUSSIE was born in Gonder, Ethiopia. She came to America when she was fifteen years old. Her first name means "cross" like a Christian cross in the Amharic language spoken by the Amharic in Ethiopia. This name was given to her by her mother because her mom wanted a girl child. That's why when Rodas was born she was given her special biblical name. The language that Rodas' family speaks is Amharic.

In the future Rodas hopes to be a doctor; it's what she wants to accomplish in her life. She hopes to become a doctor and then help people back in her home country. When she came to America it was summer, which meant a hot time. She couldn't even sleep all night. It was a sleepless night she will never forget. It was a struggle the whole summer because it was the first time the weather changed for her.

When Rodas thinks of her home in Ethiopia she misses *injera*, especially the way her grandmother cooked it for her when she was a little girl and her grandmother took care of her every single day. Also, her grandmother told her stories about her family tree and ancestors. Rodas' grandmother made every day fun for her because she wanted to see Rodas' face joyful. Rodas is happy she came to the USA. She is getting a good education. Rodas believes that food is life-giving energy. She also believes that if you like food, you should cook! She believes that many homeless people do not have enough food. Rodas loves the food that is cooked for Ethiopian holidays, especially when there is a lot of it, and she believes that food stands for many different cultures and countries.

SAGAR RAI was born in a refugee camp in Nepal. He speaks three languages: his first language is Nepali, his second one is Hindi and his last language is English. Sagar came to the United States on December 11, 2011. In Nepal, his house in the refugee camp was made of bamboo and often there were floods. Once a month, when the government always gave them rice and vegetables, each person got only 5 kg of rice for the month.

Sama Jabbarimehmani was born in Tehran in Iran. She lived in Turkey for three years and then moved to the USA. She can speak Farsi, Turkish, and English. Sama loves art, drawing and playing the violin. She started learning violin when she was ten years old. Her family always encourages her to learn new things. Sometimes Sama cooks when she is alone at home, but her brother loves food even more than she does and he makes new foods. Her name means "Sky."

Sama believes when she watches the stars she can achieve her wishes. She believes in miracles and that her dreams will come true. Sama believes that if she plays her violin with all of her heart then she will find great happiness and a new way to start walking toward her dreams. She believes it is important to love life and the music that shakes her bones. Sama also hopes to become a dentist.

Smile Khai was born in Myanmar, Kalaymute. He moved to Malaysia when he was nine years old. He arrived in the U.S. in 2010. He can speak Burmese, Chin, Zomi, Sezan, and English. He understands the languages of Falam, Mizo, and Karen. He dreams of graduating and becoming an actor. So therefore, he will try his best to reach his dreams.

He misses his country's fresh air because there is no other fresh air like in his country. It is air that would make you think you could fly if you closed your eyes when the fresh breezes of Myanmar came. He also misses his auntie's cooking from his country because the food from his country is the best underground food for him, and even better if his aunty is cooking it.

Smile Khai believes he can fly if he tastes a very sweet fruit which is *Ohza* from his country. He believes he will have more power if he can summon the strength of food. He believes that food can bring families together.

SOLOMON DAM (SOLO) was born in Burma. He is fifteen years old. He speaks two languages, Chin and English. He came to America in 2013. His dream is to become an engineer or soccer player but his family wants him to become an engineer.

He misses his country's food because it has tastes he will never forget. In Burma his grandma cooked for him. He and his grandma had a really big garden with different types of vegetables. Solo likes to eat vegetables, especially the corn his mom cooked for him. He knows he has a really good mom and grandma, who support him in everything he does and wants. Now in the USA, he has started to play soccer. Solo is proud to be Chin. He wants to help people. He believes that corn has the most powerful memories for him, because when he eats corn he misses his grandma.

SUSMA RAI was born in Nepal. She is eighteen years old. For fifteen years, Susma lived in a refugee camp and then moved to the United States with her whole family on November 29, 2012. She speaks three languages: Nepali, English and a little bit of Hindi. Her life in the refugee camp was very difficult in part because she could not get a quality education. When she was in Nepal there were times when she did not have enough to eat.

She misses her grandma's cooking and the way her mom grew vegetables in a garden. She believes that her aunt's own special Nepali cooking brings her back to memories of home. She believes that her mom's hands are magic in the way that she makes delicious food. Susma also believes that her mom made enough delicious food for her entire family. She believes that no one's home should be a place of hunger.

THAN WIN was born in Thailand. He came to America when he was nine years old. He lived in a refugee camp called Mae La, where he had enough to survive. His dream was to go to America one day for a better life. In 2008, his dream came true. Now in the USA, Than wants to be a police officer so he can help people. He is happy to be Karen and he is proud of his parents because they are strong and supportive. He believes that refugees should have more food, because the only things refugees eat are fruits that come from the green forests. He also believes that food can bring people together and create happiness. He understands that without enough food people can become savage and greedy.

THIN ZA AUNG (AUNG AUNG) was born in Burma, Chin State. In 2014, he arrived in the USA. There are six people in his family including himself. He has been living here for one year and now he is studying here, in the U.S. His first name means "a million of money." It is important for him. He is Christian. When he lived with his grandpa, his lovely grandpa always taught him about the Holy Bible. Now Thin Za Aung lives in the USA and his grandpa lives in Burma and he is still alive.

Thin Za Aung's favorite job is engineering. If he can become an engineer, he wants to help those who do not have enough food to eat and help orphans who have lost their parents in his homeland. He has sympathy for people. When he was seven years old his father passed away (rest in peace). Throughout his life he has struggled, until now. His mother works every Monday through Friday. Now he goes to Foster High School and he plans to go to college after he finishes high school. He is proud of his family and proud of all of his teachers in high school. He can speak more than four languages, such as Malaysian, Burmese Chin, and English. Especially, he can speak the Chin language perfectly.

He believes that food can give energy to everyone. He also believes that all people should choose which foods are the best to eat for their lives. He believes that everyone in the world should have enough food. He believes that food is very important for all people. He believes that having enough food can make a happy life for everyone and that food can give peace to everyone. Thin Za Aung also believes that his grandmother's soup makes his family happy and that food can remind all of us about our culture and traditions.

Vu Nguyen was born in Ho Chi Minh City. He likes people to call him "Joestar." He lived in Viet Nam for fourteen years and he moved to the U.S. with his dad in August of 2014. He lives with his dad and his stepmother. He speaks two languages: English and Vietnamese. He would like to learn Japanese to achieve his dream to be a Mangaka (a Japanese cartoonist) of Weekly *Shonen Jump* Magazine. He believes that food can change the human soul.

Wilbert Alexander Anaya Murcia was born in El Salvador. He came to America when he was fifteen years old in 2012. He speaks Spanish and English. His goal is to work and be prepared for the future. He misses his favorite food called pupusas, a traditional food in El Salvador. He's thankful to be in this school and he is thankful for the teachers who have helped him to learn English. He believes that governments must help people who are hungry.

Zakaria Mohamed Kahin was born in a small city in Somalia. He speaks English and Somali. Zakaria moved to the USA when he was nine years old in 2009. His dream is to become a professional soccer player. He misses the rice with meat and tomato that is part of Somali cultural food. His brother often cooked it for him. The meaning of his name is "helpful and kind." His hopes and goals are to graduate school and have a better future. He is proud of being in the USA and getting a good education. Zakaria believes refugees should have more food. He also believes food can bring people together.

ZUNG TIN MAWI was born in Khampat, Burma. She went to Malaysia in 2008 and she came to America in 2012. She can speak three languages, Chin Hakha, Burmese and Falam. Her religion is Christian. Zung's hopes and dreams are to become a singer and to protect her family.

Zung's mother cooked food that she misses from her country. Zung believes that food gives us energy so that we have strength to work or cook. Zung also believes that every parent should not let their children remain hungry if at all possible.

Acknowledgements

We wish to thank the following organizations for their financial support:

The Association for Business Communication, JIM DUBINSKY, Executive Director
The Foster High School Administration, PAT LARSEN, Principal
KBCS FM Radio
King County 4Culture
Shunpike
Tukwila School District Administration, DR. NANCY COOGAN, Superintendent
Tukwila School District ELL Services, LILYA STEFOGLO, Department Head

Our appreciation goes to the following individuals for their generous in-kind donations and project support:

KAORI BRAND, Documentary Film-maker
CLAUDIA CASTRO LUNA, Seattle's First Civic Poet, who visited our classroom
CARRIE CURLEY, United Reprographics, Graphic Designer, for project posters and her eternal project support
DAVID LYNCH, Incomparable Project Photographer, for students' and Project Feast cooks' portraits
ERIC MEDALLE, Graphic Designer for Stories of Arrival logo
TOM PRUIKSMA, Poet, Magician, Translator
RICHARD ROGERS, Graphic Designer, for poetry posters and his over the top generosity
SAM VERHOVEK, Foster High School News and Publicity

Our collaboration with PROJECT FEAST would not have been possible without the efforts and vision of ALANNA MCDONALD, former Project Feast Program and Event Manager, MARGARET MAJOR, AmeriCorps VISTA Program Coordinator and the enthusiastic support of Project Feast Founder and Executive Director, VEENA PRASAD. We also extend our thanks to KATHLEEN FLINN, for her wonderful recipe writing workshop when we visited Project Feast and to the eight PROJECT FEAST COOKS who our students interviewed and the generosity of their time and their thoughtful answers: SUSANA ACA, TAGHREED IBRAHIM, TAGHREED MAHMOOD, NAFFIE SINYAN, YNGRID SOLIS, INNA STETSENKO, NEBIAT YIFRU and YANZHI ZHANG.

(continued next page)

Finally, our gratitude goes to our longstanding project partners, The Institute for Poetic Medicine (IPM) in Palo Alto, CA and Seattle's Jack Straw Cultural Center.

We are honored to be an IPM Poetry Partner Project. Under the auspices of the IPM, we receive funds from a Kalliopeia Foundation grant. IPM has given generous support to our project from its inception. JOHN FOX, the IPM founder and director has been a continual inspiration to us with his passion for poetry and his wise counsel as to the importance of writing from the heart. Our partnership with the IPM has granted us national recognition on their website and in the IPM on-line Poetic Medicine Journal. The zeal for our project from John and the IPM board of directors has been a key aspect in sustaining our project.

JOAN RABINOWITZ, the Executive Director, of Seattle's Jack Straw Cultural Center has championed and supported our project with her life-long commitment to promoting cross cultural arts and understandings and with her enthusiasm for this joint endeavor. Along with Joan, we also thank vocal coaches MEG McLYNN, ANDREW McGINN, and GIN HAMMOND; sound engineers, DANIEL GUENTHER and TOM STILES; program assistants LEAH MEYER and JOSH KORNBLUH; radio producer and web designer, LEVI FULLER; and photographer, SHERWIN ENG. Our field trips to Seattle's Jack Straw Cultural Center took place over two days during the project. The voice recording is an essential aspect of our project since bringing voices and visibility to the community are central to our project. Our partnership with Jack Straw provides our students with the unique benefit of individual vocal coaching, given with care and meticulous attention toward bringing their poems from the page to the spoken word.

Our field trip days to Jack Straw are a highlight of our entire project. They are a turning point for the students, allowing them to experience the power of their voices as nothing else can. Besides our field trip to Jack Straw, three of their recording engineers brought their equipment to Project Feast and recorded the interviews our students conducted with Project Feast cooks. Through our partnership with Jack Straw we receive generous financial support from the National Endowment for the Arts, the WA State Arts Commission and individual donors.

From Our Partners

Notes from:
the Institute for Poetic Medicine,
Jack Straw Cultural Center,
and Project Feast

From the Institute for Poetic Medicine:

IN A WORLD where we know all too well about adults who behave badly—who act without concern, or worse, willingly cause deprivation and suffering to people, to children and to our planet—I nurture in my heart a persistent conviction that organizations like the Stories of Arrival: Youth Voices Poetry Project and Project Feast make a difference.

The difference made is lasting because it is generative.

What is more generative than a garden? The garden, with its call for attention and patience, will bless us again and then again with bounty and beauty.

What lasts more than the poem? A poem, that entered ages ago into the marrow of our bones, reminds us. I have spoken to elders who struggle with dementia but who will remember flawlessly every single word of the poem learned in childhood.

Delicious food prepared and cooked with love, grows and sustains our bodies—we see this especially in children, but this is what we all require to live. Poetry is necessary too; the lines of a poem are food for our soul.

Stories of Arrival and Project Feast are motivated by something more than themselves—by tradition and a creative spark, by the abundant earth and the ineluctable human heart.

My great appreciation goes to the project co-directors. Merna Ann Hecht, poet and teaching artist, for her profound dedication and remarkable sensitivity to this work of poetry-as-healer. And to Carrie Stradley, Foster ELL classroom teacher, whose unstinting joy and attention is given day after day, year after year to these young people.

I truly believe by creating *Our Table of Memories,* the contributions of all participants and collaborators, particularly of the poets and cooks, create a world that is loving, meaningful and lasting. The world we want to live in.

—JOHN FOX, Founder, The Institute for Poetic Medicine

From Project Feast:

IT HAS BEEN AN HONOR to participate in the Stories of Arrival Project alongside such creative, compassionate, and courageous youth, teachers and artists. Engaging the voices of both refugee and immigrant youth from Foster High School, and Project Feast program participants created an invaluable opportunity to explore the power of food and poetry in discovering, celebrating, and sharing who we are.

While our participants have shared their stories with one another during training programs, as well as with the broader Seattle community through cooking classes and catering events, the opportunity to share their journeys as immigrants and cooks with young people in their community on a similar journey was a truly unique and empowering mentorship experience.

From hosting the recipe-writing workshop at our headquarters at the Tukwila Community Center, to being the guests of the Foster students as they shared their poems and family dishes, each step in the making of this book has reaffirmed the importance of food as an expression of identity and as a platform for cross-cultural understanding.

We thank the Foster students for their courage and generosity in sharing their stories with the Project Feast community, and for reminding us of the incredible power of youth voices to inspire and shape the world we live in.

—MARGARET MAJOR, AmeriCorps VISTA Program Coordinator, Project Feast

From Jack Straw Cultural Center:

Spices and foods, cultural traditions and identity, combine in a variety of tastes and smells that make cooking and the resulting array of flavors something very special to share and experience. I continue to be entranced by the magic that comes from these students' words, drawn from them so lovingly by Merna and Carrie and their courage to share their thoughts out loud. The students and the teachers, artists, and partner organizations that work with them and make this program happen, is a very special group. I'm honored that we are a part of it.

—Joan Rabinowitz, Executive Director, Jack Straw Cultural Center

www.jackstraw.org/programs/ed/youth/foster.shtml

Merna Ann Hecht

A nationally known storyteller, a frequent conference presenter, and a published poet and essayist, Merna also teaches Creative Writing and Humanities for the University of WA, Tacoma. As a recipient of a 2008 National Storytelling Network Brimstone Award for Applied Storytelling, she worked at BRIDGES: A Center for Grieving Children in Tacoma. Based on that experience and her work with young refugees and immigrants since founding and co-directing the Stories of Arrival Poetry Project, her writing and teaching most often focus on the necessity of bringing creative arts to settings for young people who have experienced trauma and loss.

In over thirty years of working as a teaching artist Merna is continually touched by the complex beauty and vulnerability that comes forth when people are given the space for telling their stories. She finds sustenance in the common language of food and poetry as evidenced in the poems within these pages. In times of deep concern about human rights and basic human needs lacking for many worldwide, the Stories of Arrival poets inspire her with their spirit of hope and their will and actions toward peacemaking. Though heartily engaged in her work, not a week passes without conjuring something from scratch in her kitchen, most often with cinnamon and rarely without garlic or butter.

Carrie Stradley

For over 15 years Carrie Stradley has dedicated her career to the empowerment of youth as an English Language Learning teacher. Passionate about guiding students through the gauntlet of the English language, she aims to empower them so they may find their voice and move confidently into their chosen futures. She finds working with youth incredibly fulfilling and appreciates their unique perspective on the world. A National Board Certified Teacher, Carrie has worked in various capacities over the years as a member of standards review committees through the Washington State Office of the Superintendent, a guest lecturer at the University of Washington, and as an advocate for the families of her students. When not devouring all things education, Carrie is often caught staring longingly at a framed map of the world in her dining room, and feels it is necessary to keep her passport up-to-date and at hand at all times. She believes whole-heartedly in the power of food to heal both body and spirit, and prefers to use chicken feet wrapped in fresh dill when concocting nourishing bowls of broth to feed her family.

Index
of poets by first name

Index
of Project Feast cooks by first name

CPSIA information can be obtained
at www.ICGtesting.com
Printed in the USA
FSOW03n0052020316
17569FS